TAPESTRY WITH
PULLED WARP

TAPESTRY WITH
PULLED WARP

Inspiration, Technique, and the Creative Process

Susan Iverson

SCHIFFER
CRAFT
4880 Lower Valley Road • Atglen, PA 19310

Designed by Ashley Millhouse
Cover design by Ashley Millhouse
Front cover photos by Katherine Wetzel
Type set in AWConqueror Std Inline/Effra

ISBN: 978-0-7643-6760-1
Printed in China

Published by Schiffer Craft
An imprint of Schiffer Publishing, Ltd.
4880 Lower Valley Road
Atglen, PA 19310
Phone: (610) 593-1777; Fax: (610) 593-2002
Email: Info@schifferbooks.com
Web: www.schifferbooks.com

For our complete selection of fine books on this and related subjects, please visit our website at www.schifferbooks.com. You may also write for a free catalog.

Schiffer Publishing's titles are available at special discounts for bulk purchases for sales promotions or premiums. Special editions, including personalized covers, corporate imprints, and excerpts, can be created in large quantities for special needs. For more information, contact the publisher.

We are always looking for people to write books on new and related subjects. If you have an idea for a book, please contact us at proposals@schifferbooks.com.

OTHER SCHIFFER CRAFT BOOKS ON RELATED SUBJECTS:

Anatomy of a Tapestry: Techniques, Materials, Care, Jean Pierre Larochette and Yadin Larochette, Illustrations by Yael Lurie, ISBN 978-0-7643-5933-0

Weaving Patterned Bands: How to Create and Design with 5, 7, and 9 Pattern Threads, Susan J. Foulkes, ISBN 978-0-7643-5550-9

Tapestry Design Basics and Beyond: Planning and Weaving with Confidence, Tommye McClure Scanlin, foreword by Rebecca Mezoff, 978-0-7643-6156-2

For my parents, who always encouraged my life in the arts

WHAT IS PULLED WARP?

Pulled warp is a term for a technique that allows a weaver to create a tapestry that curves, bends, or becomes three-dimensional without cutting or stitching. Simply put, specific areas of the warp are left unwoven. When the tapestry is taken off the loom, the warp in the unwoven areas is pulled through the woven areas and out at the top or bottom edges of the tapestry.

MY ROMANCE WITH WEAVING AND WITH PULLED WARP

I fell in love with weaving at Colorado State University (CSU), where I studied with Sherri Smith in the early 1970s. While I had gone to school for the love of painting (and skiing), I took weaving as a sophomore studio elective, and there was no turning back. Weaving seemed to offer pure potential as an art form, as old as time but also cutting edge. From Sherri I learned to think deeply about textile structure and the power of taking chances with technique—the "What if?" method of working. After two years of investigating complex weaves, I discovered tapestry. I found that it provided an object/image conversation that was exactly what I had been searching for in my work. The most basic of weaves, it produced a fabric that fully engaged my imagination. At CSU I developed my love of creating and a strong work ethic in tandem.

In 1973 I moved to Philadelphia for two intensive years of graduate study at the Tyler School of Art at Temple University. Here is where I would begin my long interest in manipulating tapestry, when I was fortunate enough to see *The Yellow Braid* by Herman Scholten in person on a field trip to New York City. I then purchased *Beyond Craft: The Art Fabric* by Jack Lenor Larsen and Mildred Constantine, which had an entire chapter on this Dutch artist. There were a couple of small sketches included in this influential and timeless book that provided clues as to how Scholten may have worked. The idea of curving a woven fabric, apparently achieved without cutting or sewing, was so intriguing. Scholten's tapestries, which appeared completely honest and uncontrived, were technical mysteries to me and to the other graduate students in fiber. Along with our professor, Adela Akers, we worked to solve this exciting technical problem. There was a buzz of excitement in the fiber studio as different students talked about possible ways to alter the form of a tapestry. It became clear that leaving open warp in some areas and closing that area after the tapestry came off the loom was a reasonable solution. John McQueen, one of my fellow graduate students in the program, then wove a wonderful tapestry of handspun white wool that spiraled multiple times with a layer of burrs in between each layer of weaving to form an intriguing object. In the late 1970s, Adela Akers wove a beautiful series of ocean-referenced tapestries that used pulled warp to create undulating, three-dimensional surfaces.

After growing up in Wisconsin and living in Colorado, the move to the East Coast was a visual and cultural shock. I missed the open fields and rolling hills of central Wisconsin and the mountains of Colorado, but I loved the architecture and energy of Philadelphia. The faculty and other students at Tyler were important to the development of how I saw myself within the art world. The proximity to NYC allowed me to see exciting exhibitions of the newest work, and the museum visits brought to life the work I had studied in many art history courses.

Beyond Craft: The Art Fabric. This influential book by Mildred Constantine and Jack Leonor Larsen has a full chapter on the work of Herman Scholten.

In 1975 I graduated from Tyler, taught two summer courses at the Kansas City Art Institute, packed up my few possessions (including my new Gilmore loom) from Madison, and then moved to Richmond, Virginia, for a teaching position at Virginia Commonwealth University (VCU). I dove into full-time teaching and research. I found that I loved sharing information with the students, who were so full of enthusiasm and energy. I wove a lot of tapestries during these early years that investigated the physicality of tapestry. My ideas didn't require using the pulled warp technique at that time. I was able to use layering and some shaping to bring my ideas to life.

I didn't have a need for the pulled warp technique until 1978 or 1979, when I started work on a series of large tapestries in the shape of Xs and Vs. The Xs were simply made of two crossed strips, but I wanted the V shape to be one continuous panel, and that meant using pulled warp. The first V I tried was almost 6' tall, and that meant weaving a strip 12' long with a very, very large triangle of open warp in the middle. I started with great enthusiasm, since this would be my first large-scale, pulled warp

Adela Akers. *Summer and Winter*, 1977. Tapestry, 84" × 72" × 10". *Courtesy of the artist*

Susan Iverson / John Hawthorne, 1981, exhibition in the ICA gallery of the Virginia Museum of Fine Arts. *Courtesy of VMFA Photo Archives, © Virginia Museum of Fine Arts*

tapestry. Everything went well until I got it off the loom and onto the finishing table, ready to pull the open warp. This was one of the biggest learning experiences of my life. It was a disaster. I quickly realized that it had been completely foolish of me to think that it was physically possible to pull a warp through several feet of woven tapestry. Simply put, there was too much friction to achieve the goal. At one hilarious point I had John Hawthorne, a friend/colleague and wonderful artist, lie down on the tapestry to hold it in place on the work table while I gripped a warp with a pair of pliers and pulled with all my might. It did not move. I learned a great deal about pulled warp with that tapestry, and I will explain the solution to "big pulls" later in this book. I do appreciate mistakes that turn into major teaching/learning moments, and this moment taught me a great deal about the need to think more carefully and plan ahead for the pulling process!

Over the years I wove more and more technical samples of pulled warp and eventually added this technique to my tapestry-weaving classes at VCU. It gave the students more options if they were interested in

John Hawthorne and Susan Iverson in photograph for the 1981 exhibition. *Photo by William Hammersley*

The talented and productive class members from the Pushing Tapestry class at Penland School of Craft

dimensional work. As with any technique, most students merely added it to their technical toolbox and moved on, but a few students totally embraced it and wove some wonderfully inventive projects. I taught a few pulled warp workshops around the country and always enjoyed the engagement with weavers who were open to new possibilities. In 2018 I was privileged to teach a two-week class at the Penland School of Craft in North Carolina that covered pulled warp and other shaping techniques for tapestry. The class was energetic, productive, and memorable. It was one of those wonderful classes with a perfect mix of students who supported and fed off each other in creative ways.

Each of the series I have worked with over my career has been based on what I was obsessed with at the time. A new interest grows in my sketchbook for quite a while before it blooms into work that needs to be woven. I

have generally stayed with each series for three to seven years. I always move on to a new series before I feel that I have fully completed the previous series. It is a balancing act. I never tried to force pulled warp onto a series, since it is simply a tool that is necessary for some ideas, and not for others. However, I am always excited when I realize that it will be an aspect of some new work. I have completed almost 50 tapestries using pulled warp, many of them from the *Horizon* series, woven between 1997 and 2002. I don't believe I will ever get over my fascination for the potential that pulled warp provides in developing ideas for tapestry.

I was pleased, energized, and a bit terrified when I realized that I was ready to make the commitment to write a book about pulled warp. It is an honor to have the opportunity to share with you some of the knowledge I have gathered.

WAYS TO USE THIS BOOK

This book may be used in many ways by weavers and art lovers. It was conceived as a way to ensure that this fairly obscure technique could be easily learned by tapestry weavers, from novice to expert, now and far into the future. While I do not presume that a weaver could not figure out the technique on their own, I believe this book is a good reference for quick learning. I have included enough technical images so that even if you choose not to read all my words, you will still be able to get the basic gist of the process. I have, however, included a lot of worthwhile hints, warnings of pitfalls, and maybe even some sage advice in the instructions. Forty years of teaching studio art at a university provided me with a fairly accurate understanding of how visual artists accumulate technical information. I have included specific instructions in the beginning sections for step-by-step learning and reminders of some of the crucial steps throughout the book. I then rely on the reader to have absorbed the basic information and to be able to use that knowledge as they progress further through the book.

If you are fairly new to tapestry weaving, you will find easy-to-understand directions for the samples, along with numerous images that support the written information. This book should be seen as your companion at the work table and at the loom. It will guide you through every step, making it possible for you to succeeded beautifully with each sample you choose to weave.

More-advanced weavers, or those who have already tried this technique, may be able to pick and choose which samples to try instead of starting at the beginning. It is important that all levels of weavers carefully prepare the pattern and maquette for each sample they are going to weave. It is through this process that you will fully understand what is structurally happening.

For those readers who have experimented quite a bit with pulled warp, you will get the most new information from the chapter on complex pulls. You may also feel compelled to try one of the samples that you have not yet woven, or to devise a new sample that combines one or more of the simple samples. I am a firm believer that you can't weave too many samples!

With encouragement, this book also became an exploration of my work and how I have used the pulled warp technique, off and on, throughout my entire career. I have included a fair amount of information about my creative process, why I work in series, and why I choose pulled warp for some tapestries and not others. I hope this information will be of interest to weavers, to artists working in other media, and also to people who just love looking at and living with art.

If you are like me, you will flip through the book looking for images that speak to you on some level. While the technical information is presented in a predominantly linear manner, the aesthetic information is shared more organically. I hope you will find many things within these pages that will engage your imagination.

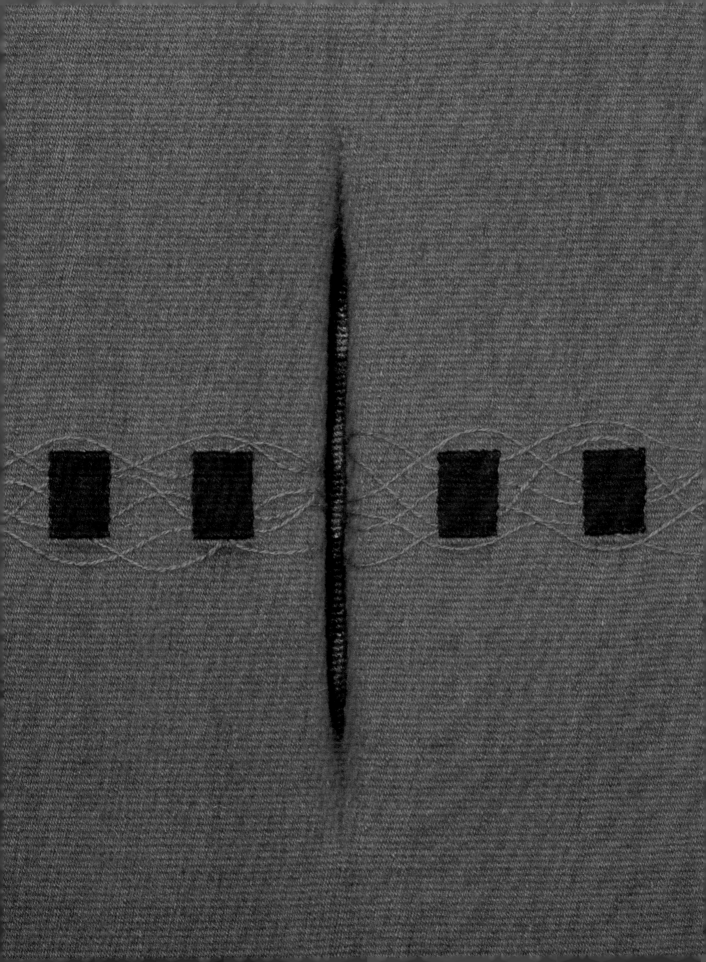

CHAPTER 1

FLAT CURVES AND ANGLES

CHAPTER 1

FLAT CURVES AND ANGLES

CHAPTER 1

FLAT CURVES AND ANGLES

Setting Up Your Loom for the Samples

This book assumes that you know how to dress a loom and the basics of weaving. If you need assistance with this, I recommend the following books: *Learning to Weave* by Deborah Chandler for dressing a floor loom or *The Art of Tapestry Weaving* by Rebecca Mezoff for the use of vertical or frame looms. Please remember that a loom's purpose is to simply support, space, and tension the warp. Our ancestors made do with two sticks!

LOOM

A tapestry with pulled warp may be woven on any floor, tapestry, or frame loom that you are comfortable using. Many of the samples shown in this book are woven on a Gilmore floor loom, which is my loom of choice. I've been weaving on this loom for over 40 years, and it is my best friend. When I teach workshops on the pulled warp technique, the students generally use a simple frame loom or a tapestry loom.

WARP

The warp should be strong and smooth. ABSOLUTELY NO KNOTS. Knots will cause serious problems during the pulling process. For best possible results, use linen or cotton for your first sample. Once you fully understand this technique, you can experiment with different warps and wefts. I use an 8/4 linen with good results. Many tapestry weavers use cotton seine twine. I would suggest a 12/9 or 12/12.

You will notice in the technical images that I have dyed the linen I am using a medium gray. This is my preference. A bonus to using a darker warp is that if any tiny bit of warp is visible after the tapestry is woven and pulled, the warp will look like a shadow.

Weaving on my Gilmore loom. *Photo by Edward Parsons*

A frame loom with multiple narrow warps of 3/2 perle cotton sett at 8 epi. The warp on the metal bars will be a three-selvedge tapestry when the bottom bar is pulled out.

WEFT

I recommend that you use wool weft for your first samples. Wool will be easy to use, since it is the most "forgiving" of the fibers. Most of the samples in this book are woven with two- or three-ply wools that run from 750 to 1,000 yards per pound. Collingwood rug wool is a good choice. Harrisonville Highland wool will also work quite nicely for these samples, as will bundles of finer wools. I dye most of my own yarns and currently use Henry's Attic Crown Colony two-ply wool.

I recommend that you wash all the fibers that you use. This will make sure that the yarn is clean, and it will also restore the round shape to the yarn if it has been tightly compressed on a cone or tube. If you are using good-quality tapestry yarns, this might not be strictly necessary. I have never been sorry that I spent the extra time preparing my yarns for weaving. I have had students who were quite sorry when, for example, a weft yarn bled when the tapestry was blocked.

WARP SETT AND LENGTH

The samples are sett at 6 warp ends per inch (epi) unless otherwise noted. This is my strong recommendation for beginning. While this technique can be woven at any sett, with the appropriate yarns, it is important that after the weaving process the warp can be easily pulled through the warp "tunnel" without too much friction. There is an easy way to decide if your warp sett and weft size are compatible for this technique. Simply insert the weft yarn between two warps on the loom. The yarn should fit easily between the warps and not push them apart.

The length of the warp will depend on your loom. If you are using a frame loom, you will be setting up the loom separately for each sample or pair of samples. The woven length of this first sample should be about 6", and you will need about 4"–6" of unwoven warp on each end in order to easily pull the warp once it comes off the loom.

If you are setting up on a floor loom, you should put on 8 or 9 feet of warp to weave the first three samples.

I know some of you may be much more comfortable weaving at 8 epi. This book is a guide, so if you are an expert tapestry weaver who weaves at a finer sett, then alter the size of your warp and weft for this.

Hint: Weave two samples of the same shape at the same time, one to pull and one to keep as a pattern/example; or weave one sample and photocopy it before you do the pull to document the exact size of the sample. You really will find having these examples very helpful in the future.

Making the Pattern for Your First Sample

Always make a pattern for your pulled warp tapestries. This technique can be counterintuitive, so you want to make sure that what you are planning will actually work. The pattern will define all the areas that are woven and those that remain unwoven. I always make a small pattern that is also used for the small maquette (model) to test the idea, and then I make a full-size pattern, which can be used as the cartoon and as the full-size maquette for all my work based on that pattern. For these samples your original pattern will be the same size as the weaving.

A major part of pulled warp involves experimenting with pattern making. The pattern for this first simple sample will be straightforward. I generally work with graph paper for small samples like this, but lined or unlined paper will also work well.

YOUR FIRST PATTERN: A FLAT, SIMPLE CURVE

Cut a 3" wide strip of paper 6" or 7" long. Your sample will be 3" wide. The 6" to 7" represents the woven length of the sample before it is pulled.

Draw out three symmetrical triangles (isosceles) that are 3" wide, going from edge to edge of the paper, and 1⅛" high on the right side. These are called darts and relate closely to the darts used in sewing garments. Photocopy or re-draw this twice so you have two flat copies for later use.

The center line of the dart (triangle) for a flat sample must be perpendicular to the warp. Note that the center line in the drawing is marked by a dotted line. This ensures that when the warp is pulled, the two edges that merge are the same length, and your sample will stay flat.

Cut out the triangles but don't cut through the left edge—stop about ⅛" short.

Close the top triangle, matching the two long edges, and use a small piece of tape to secure it. Notice that the paper bends but stays flat. If it sticks up a bit at the bend, simply press it down with your fingers.

Close the other two triangles and tape closed. This is the maquette and what our first sample will look like when woven!

The cartoon for weaving will be one of the photocopies of the pattern.

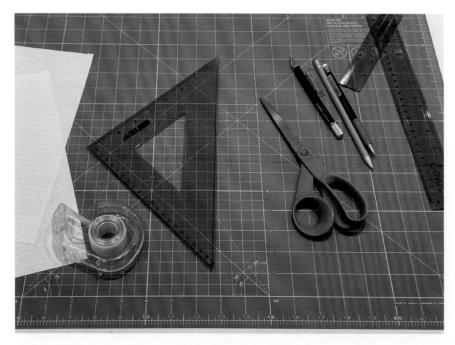

What you may need for making a pattern

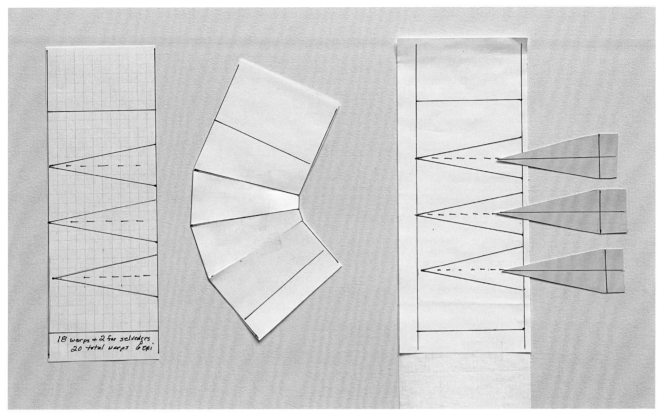

18 warps + 2 for selvedgers
20 total warps 6 epi

Pattern, maquette, cartoon for weaving, and spacers

Alternative Way to Make a Curved Pattern

This is the method I prefer, since you can easily evaluate the curve during the process of cutting and taping. It is a more spontaneous method:

- Use lined or graph paper.

- Cut out a 3" wide strip.

- About 2" from one end, cut a horizontal slit from the right side to the left —be careful not to cut through the left edge.

- Slide the two edges over each other until you have the angle you desire, and tape the center of the overlap.

- Repeat this process until you have the curve you desire.

- Using a straightedge, mark the center line of each angle with a pen or pencil and then cut along that line, being careful not to cut through the left edge.

- Straighten the left edge of the strip and you will see that there is now an open triangular space, and both long edges of the triangle are the same length.

Spacers are what we will use to hold the non-woven areas open during the weaving process. The spacers will be the same shape as the triangles but will be made about ½" wider than the woven strip. You can trace one of the cut-out triangles onto a piece of heavier paper or use a ruler and draw out the triangles onto the heavier paper. I like to use tagboard or manilla folders, but you can be creative with this, and even postcards work well. Don't use anything too heavy or it will not go around the loom's beams if you are using a floor loom.

Cut six identical spacers for your two samples.

Note: Yarn may be used as a filler instead of a spacer, but it is time consuming to weave and remove. I do not generally recommend this.

For really large darts, you will want to cut your spacers along the center line and hinge them with tape to allow them to bend more easily as the tapestry goes around the front beam and cloth beam of your floor loom. If you are using a frame loom, this is not necessary.

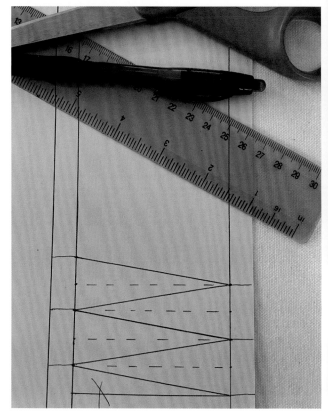

Make your spacers carefully.

Additional Information about Patterns

- Interfacing that is printed with a grid can work well for large patterns.

- The center of a dart must be perpendicular to the warp, and the two edges of the dart are the same length.

- For flat curves the dart should go from selvedge to selvedge, or one or two warps short of that. If it doesn't, the tapestry will become dimensional.

- For smooth curves, use several small darts.

- For angles, use one large dart.

- For dimensional tapestry the darts may not go from selvedge to selvedge.

- When the two edges of the dart are not the same length, the surface will ripple and the pull may become problematic or impossible.

- If your pattern doesn't do what you want it to do, neither will the weaving. Paper does bend differently than tapestry, but not too differently. Paper provides a reasonable representation.

- Your imagination, while wonderful, does not replace a pattern.

Simple Curve Sample

Wind a warp for two 3" wide strips, with two warps running together on each selvedge. Setting the warp at 6 epi, you will need a total of 40 warp ends. This is assuming that you will be weaving two side-by-side samples as I recommend for the first small samples. If you choose to weave only one sample, then you will need 20 warp ends.

Dress your loom, leaving 1"–2" between the strips. Remember to double your outside warps. Weave enough header to make sure that the warp is running perfectly straight. My headers are usually ½" or more. If you are on a loom with a reed, each warp should be "floating" in its dent without touching the metal. Please note that the pulled warp technique requires very careful weaving, so that each warp runs in a perfectly straight line throughout. This is not difficult, but it does take patience and practice. The more carefully you do each step of a process allows the following step to be easier. You will have a better outcome if you complete each and every step with care.

Start the wefts for each strip on the same edge. On the floor loom, weave one weft row on each strip and beat in. If you are using a frame loom without a shedding devise, you may want to weave up several rows on one strip and then the same number on the other. Keep your selvedges straight and remember to use enough weft in each row to go over and under the warp without pulling in your selvedges. Adjust your weft "bubbles" to ensure a smooth tapestry with no draw-in.

Beat your tapestry in firmly. The weave needs to be firm enough so that when the sample is off the loom, these woven areas will not compress further during the pulling process.

Continue weaving up to where the first angle begins, and then you will start weaving over and under fewer warps to achieve an accurate angle. Notice that on my sample, the angle works nicely when I step back my weaving by two warps each row. This is a low angle, and to get the smoothest angle possible I turn my weft on the "valley" warps.

When you look at a row of weaving, you will notice that on every other warp you will see more warp or less warp. We will refer to the warps that are less visible as

Loom dressed to weave two side-by-side samples

Bubble the weft to ensure adequate weft in each row of weaving.

The bottom angle of your first dart

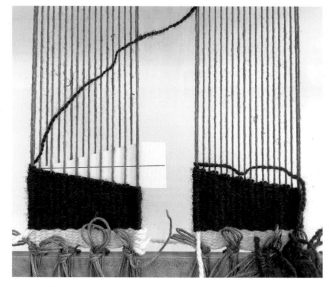

Insert the spacer; the weft wraps once around the outside warp and then weaves on top of the spacer.

If you are weaving two samples, it will be easier to fill in one side at a time.

hills, and the warps that are more visible are valleys. To make the smoothest low angles, you should turn your weft on the valley warps. When you have a steeper angle, this isn't as important. Continue weaving the angle until you reach the last warp.

Your last row of weaving below the dart and the first row on top of the dart will be in opposite sheds. This allows the two rows to fit together when you pull the open warps to close the dart.

Insert the spacer in the same shed as the last row of weaving.

Wrap the weft once around the outside, doubled warp, and you are ready to weave back across to the right with the same sequence you used to weave the angle. Beating will now be more delicate, and since the spacer is in place, you will not be able to use the beater on your floor loom. Simply push the weft into place with your fingers or a tapestry fork. If you push down too hard, the spacer will try to "squirt" out to the left. If that happens, it is easy to fix by using your fingers to push the weft up far enough to get the spacer back into its proper position. Hold the spacer in place with one hand and use the other hand to slide the weft back on top of the spacer and continue weaving. You may have to repeat this several times. This is not difficult, and there is no real trick to it; just be patient and careful.

Follow the diagram and weave several rows from selvedge to selvedge, depending on your cartoon, before starting your next angle.

Be very careful to make sure your warps are still running perfectly straight. Do not pull in your warp! I can't say this enough. Every weaver needs to unweave and reweave. I do it all the time. Try to visually check your weaving every couple of rows so you never need to take out too much. If it is worth weaving, it is worth weaving correctly.

Second spacers in place and ready to weave on top of the spacers

Continue until you have all three darts woven, then weave an inch or so going from selvedge to selvedge.

Weave in a header, just as you did at the beginning. Congratulations! You are now ready to cut your samples off the loom. When you do this, make sure that you leave at least 4" of unwoven warp at each end and leave the headers in place.

Photocopy the sample for your records. A black-and-white copy is just fine. This is not mandatory, but it is always nice to have a record of your work in the actual scale of the sample. Obviously this will only work for small samples. You may also want to take photos of the process as you go along.

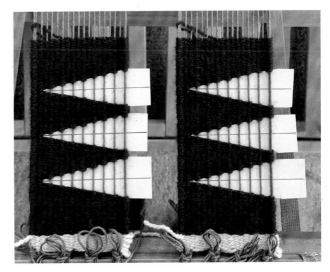

The weaving is complete except for the headers. You can see that I weave my weft tails back across two or three warps under the last weft row

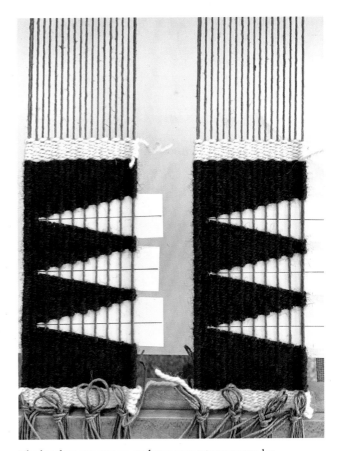

The headers are woven, and you can cut your samples off the loom.

25

Note: After I remove a tapestry from the loom, I tie two or three adjacent warps together with a simple tie to hold the headers firm against the weaving. This will keep the weft from expanding out as it relaxes after being cut off the loom. Your sample is not really fragile—but be nice to it. Lay it on a clean, flat surface until you are ready for the pulling process. Note that in some cases, you may want to tie each pair of warps together for more security during the pulling process.

Pulling the warp is exciting. Enjoy this excitement and then stay calm and relaxed during this process.

Lay the tapestry flat on a table, right side up. I cover my work tables with fabric, either canvas or duck; this provides a little "tooth" to the flat surface, which helps hold the tapestry in place while I am working on it. This certainly isn't a requirement, more of a preference, and I have found it really helpful.

Because this is a small sample, and your first sample, it's a good idea to tie each two adjacent warps on the edge away from you together in a simple tie. This will keep you from accidentally pulling a warp completely out of the weaving during the next step. Yes, this has happened. Not to me, but to more than one overeager student in a pulled warp workshop. This may seem overly cautious for some weavers, so use your best judgment.

Now you need to plan the sequence for this pull. You have three darts, and generally you want the opportunity to pull the warp in both directions. First you will pull the warp from the center dart to the front dart. Then the warp in the front dart can be pulled out from the front hem edge. It is easiest to pull toward yourself, so the next step would be to turn the sample around, and the warp from the remaining dart can be pulled out through the other hem edge, which is now closest to you. This is your plan of action, and you are ready to pull the warp.

Samples on work table and ready to pull

Start the pull with the outside doubled warp and work toward the other side. *Photo by Edward Parsons*

The open space closes as each warp is pulled.

Leave the header in place and remove the first and second spacers. Keep the sample flat on the table as you work.

Arrange the tapestry so that the two edges of the center dart are together. The excess warp will now be sticking up on top of the tapestry.

You will be using one hand to pull the warp and the other hand to hold the tapestry carefully in place. This will also allow you to feel the warp moving inside the warp tunnel as you pull. You want to feel physically connected to the tapestry. Start from the right side, which has the most open warp. Carefully take hold of the outside double warp in the dart closest to you, and pull that warp until the loop of excess warp disappears from the center dart. Do not overpull!

Repeat the pulling sequence across until all the warps from the center dart have disappeared. It is easy to pull the longer warps but more difficult to pull the warps near the point of the dart. I use needlenose pliers to grab ahold of the warp when my fingers won't fit into the space. You may need to go back and gently pull some of the warps if you can still see a bit of the warp showing through. The tapestry should still be flat.

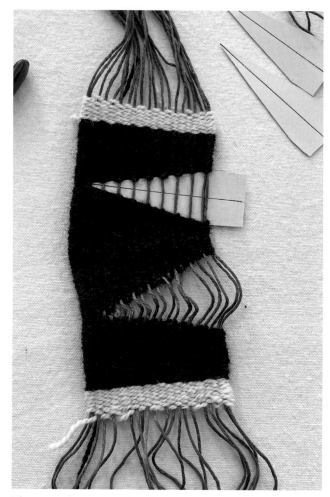

When you get close to the center of the dart, you may need to use needlenose pliers to grasp the warp. *Photo by Edward Parsons*

The center dart is now closed.

Now you can untie any warps on the hem edge nearest to you and arrange the tapestry so that the two edges of the front dart are together. Again, the excess warp will loop up on the surface.

Pull these warp loops out through the hem edge in the same way you did the first pull. The header is still in place and is helping to keep your weft yarns compressed.

The warps can now be pulled out through the hem edge.
Photo by Edward Parsons

Turn the sample around so that the other hem edge is facing you. You now have the opportunity to tighten the center dart if it needs it. After you pull out the final spacer, you can gently pull on any warps that are still visible in the middle of the center dart. If that center dart looks perfect, you can move ahead and pull the last dart closed. Again, push the two edges of the open dart together and pull each warp out through the hem edge. The header stays in place.

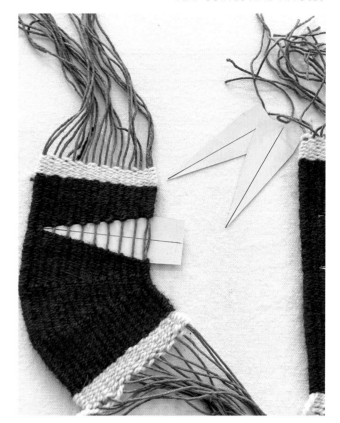

Two of the three darts are now pulled.

Turn the sample around. Start the pull on the left edge.
Photo by Edward Parsons

You have now completed pulling the first sample. Congratulations!

Later in the book we will cover finishing techniques for the weft and warp ends. I consider a sample to be just that, an example of a specific technique, and I seldom finish the warp edges, unless I want to test a particular finishing technique. You should again tie some warps together to temporarily secure the hem edge and prevent weft expansion.

Pull each warp out through the hem edge. *Photo by Edward Parsons*

The pulled sample and its unpulled twin

What if you make the darts dramatically different sizes?

What if you space the darts at different distances from each other?

What if you have 20 darts in a row and close to each other?

What if you have 20 darts in a row, and some are close and some are far apart?

What if you appliqué a curve onto another tapestry?

General Rules for Pulling Warp

Always plan out the pulling sequence before you pull any warps!

Pull firmly but gently, do not overpull. Getting the feel of the pulling process takes a little time and sensitivity. It is better to pull "not quite enough" and then go back and pull a second time.

Think about the physics of friction and pulling. It takes more effort to initiate the pull, and then almost immediately it will take less effort. You need to be very aware of this when you pull each and every warp. You need to carefully control the strength you use. The length of woven cloth that your warp is passing through will determine the effort needed.

Use both hands: one for pulling, and the other will hold the tapestry in place and feel the warp move through the fabric.

Don't move to the next pulling area until the one you are working on is perfect, unless you will also be able to pull it from the other direction. Take your time and be patient.

Because of friction, you can pull each warp only a certain distance through the woven areas. You may have to add selvedge-to-selvedge rectangular spacers every 6"–16" along the length of your tapestry, depending on your yarns and your sett. These spacers need to be tall enough that you have adequate room to grab ahold of each of the individual warps. I use selvedge-to-selvedge spacers that are about 1.5" tall. All the warps in this section will be pulled. We will talk more about this later in the book when I cover complex pulls.

The direction in which you pull can affect the look of the tapestry, since there is almost always at least some compression in the woven areas. For perfect symmetry, pull from both sides, if that is possible.

When you have several darts/spacers, you will generally start pulling from the center of the tapestry and work toward each end, just like we did on the first sample in this book.

Once you have pulled out a spacer, you must immediately complete that pull or reinsert the spacer. Remember that your weft has been compressed during the weaving process, and it will want to relax and spread out when it is not held in place by the spacer.

Take your time.

Again, always plan out the pulling sequence before you pull any warps.

Unpulling an area is not really an option.

Right Angle Sample

This sample will be very easy after you have competed the first sample. There will be one large dart that will allow the tapestry to bend at a 90-degree angle, making a corner. Of course, there are a lot of angles more than or less than 90 degrees. I recommend you weave this one because it is so recognizable—therefore it has to be precise.

Warp and weft will be the same as the first sample. You may want to change the color of weft for this sample. If you are weaving on a floor loom, you will need to tie up and re-tension your warp. If you are using a frame loom, warp it again for two 3" wide strips with double warp on the selvedges. Weave the header, making sure that your warps are evenly spaced. This sample will be about 8" long. Remember that you will need 4"–6" inches of extra warp at each end to pull the warp.

For the pattern, draw out two 3" wide strips on a piece of paper. To make your dart, draw a 90-degree angle in the middle of each strip. This means that the angle going from selvedge to selvedge is 45 degrees. The wide side of the dart will run along the right selvedge, and it should be 6" long. Like in the cartoon for your first sample, draw a dotted line from the point of the triangle/dart to the center of the right side. This will remind you to keep the center of the dart perpendicular to the warp. Photocopy this drawing of your pattern so you have a cartoon for your sample.

Cut out one of the strips for your maquette. Cut out the triangle, being careful not to cut through the left edge, and slide the two edges together to form a right angle. Tape the edges together. This is what your sample will look like after the pull.

You will make one spacer for this. It will be the size of the dart plus an additional ½" or so on the long side.

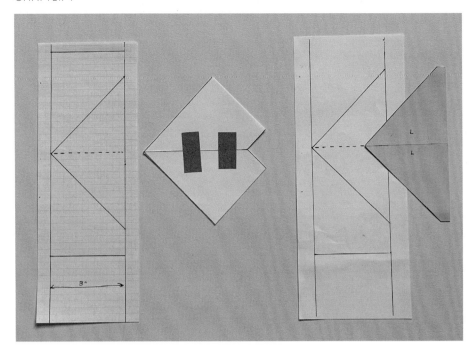

Pattern, maquette, cartoon, and spacer

Begin by weaving from selvedge to selvedge for 1". If you have adequate warp, you can, of course, weave up higher before you start the angle. The angle of this dart is much steeper than the angles in the first sample. While the dart is a 90-degree angle, each woven angle for the dart will be 45 degrees. There are several ways to determine how to weave this, so I will explain three of the easiest methods.

The first way would be to put the cartoon behind the warp and start to weave, moving over one warp to the left when you need to in order to follow the diagonal line. Remember that when you are weaving a straight diagonal line, there will be a regular sequence in the number of weft rows on each warp. That means that the sequence would be something like 2,2,2 or 2,3,2,3 but not a 1,3,2 sequence, which would give you a jagged line.

This second method is what I used. I counted up how many rows of weaving, with this yarn, it took to weave the height of the angle, which is 3". It took 45 rows. I then counted the number of warp I would be weaving with to make the angle, and that was 18 (if you have 6 dpi as I recommended). Then I divide the number of weft rows by the number of warp: 45 divided by 18 equals 2.5. This tells me that I should get a good result if I use a 2,3,2,3,2,3 sequence for how many times I weave up on a warp before I step over to the next warp to the left. If this sequence didn't work perfectly for this angle, then I would have tried a variation such as 2,2,3,2,2,3 if the first attempt was too steep or 2,3,3,2,3,3 if it was too shallow. As you can imagine, getting the angle just right will probably take some weaving, evaluating, unweaving, and reweaving.

A third, very rational and helpful way to determine the sequence would be to weave a sample with this yarn, trying different sequences to get different angles from very low to very steep. This sample would then come in handy whenever you were to use this yarn in the future. This is great advice. I have to admit that I have never done this. But, I have intended to many times, and it is a very, very good idea.

Start weaving your angle and check it with your cartoon on a regular basis. Continue weaving the angle until you get to the last warp. Wrap the weft around the outside doubled warp three times. This warp will actually bend to become the corner, which is why it gets wrapped three times, unlike in our previous samples, where the outside warp got a single wrap of weft.

Hold the cartoon behind your sample to check the angle.
Photo by Edward Parsons

Insert the spacer and weave over it.

Weave the top of the second sample if you didn't weave them at the same time.

Make your spacer and insert the spacer in the same shed as the last row of weaving, and you are ready to weave back across to the right. Since I am weaving on a floor loom, I hinged this dart by cutting it in half and taping the two halves back together. This will allow it to more easily bend around my loom's front beam. Remember that beating will now be done with more care so that you don't push the spacer out of the warp. Use the same sequence for your angle and weave across to the right until you have completed the angle. It is frequently annoying to try to keep a spacer in a large dart. Please do not try to tape it in place. You will need to keep pushing it back into position—and firmly but gently beat in the weft.

Hint—when your angle is this steep and you beat your weft carefully, you can sometimes weave without the spacer in place. You will need to insert the spacer on a regular basis to make sure you are not over-beating the weft. Then insert the spacer before you move to the selvedge-to-selvedge weaving.

When you have finished the dart, weave your tapestry selvedge to selvedge, building up 1" or more.

Weave in a header. Congratulations! You have now completed weaving your second sample. Cut the sample off the loom, leaving at least 4" of warp on each end of the sample.

Remove spacer and prepare to pull.

Move the two edges of the dart together and start the pull on the outside edge. *Photo by Edward Parsons*

Remember to tie two or three adjacent warps together with a simple tie to keep the weft from expanding out as it relaxes after being cut off the loom. Do this gently so you don't accidentally pull a warp completely out of the tapestry. Your sample is not really fragile—but remember to be nice to it. Lay it on a clean, flat surface until you are ready for the pulling process. Note that in some cases you may want to tie each pair of warps together for more security.

Remember to photocopy the sample for your records. A black-and-white copy is just fine. A copy is especially important if you have chosen to weave only a single sample.

You are ready to pull your second sample. Always stay calm and relaxed during this process.

Lay the tapestry flat on a table, right side up. As I stated earlier, I cover my work tables with fabric, either canvas or duck; this provides a little "tooth" to the flat surface, which helps hold the tapestry in place.

Since there is just one dart, there is no need to plan a sequence for the pull as we did for the first sample.

Leave the heading in place and remove the spacer. Keep the sample flat on the table as you work.

Arrange the tapestry so that the two edges of the dart are together—the excess warp will now be sticking up on top of the tapestry.

Use one hand to pull the warp and the other hand to hold the tapestry carefully in place. This will also allow you to feel the warp moving inside the warp tunnel as you pull. You want to feel physically connected to the tapestry. This will help you judge the amount of effort needed to initiate the pull on each warp and adjust your strength accordingly.

Start from the right side, which has the most open warp. Carefully take hold of the outside double warp and slowly pull that warp toward you until the loop of excess warp disappears from the dart. Pull firmly and slowly to achieve uniform tension. Do not overpull! Pull the next two or three warps.

Pull a few warps in the center of the dart. *Photo by Edward Parsons*

Finish pulling all the warps. *Photo by Edward Parsons*

Because this is a large dart, I would then pull three or four warps in the center. Repeat the pulling sequence across, in both directions, until all the warps from the dart have disappeared. You will notice that when you have to pull a warp through more woven tapestry, there is additional friction, which means more resistance when you first start pulling. You must control the strength you use when pulling. You may need to go back and gently pull some of the warps from the other side if you can still see a bit of the warp showing through the tapestry. The tapestry should still be flat.

Beautiful!

Check your angle.

Completed sample and control sample

What if you make four right angles?

What if you alternate directions of the darts and weave several right angles?

What if you wove a series of angles that looked like a tapestry electrocardiogram?

What if your flat angle is manipulated to be 3-D?

Samples should always be played with.

Compound Curve Sample

This sample is a variation on the first simple curve. This time you will weave a compound curve, using two different sizes of darts.

Now that you've completed two samples, it's time to experiment on what you have learned. This sample will be longer than the first two and involve more pulls. You can follow my directions for the cartoon, or you may also do a variation by changing the size or number of the darts.

Cut a 3" wide strip of paper for the pattern. Make this about 16" long. You may have to tape two pieces of paper together.

Draw out three triangles that have their points all facing the same selvedge, then leave about 2" before drawing four more with the points facing the other direction. Like in your first two patterns, these triangle darts should go from edge to edge of the paper. The center line of the triangle for a flat sample must be perpendicular to the warp. Note that as with the previous patterns, the center line in the drawing is marked by a dotted line. This ensures that when the warp is pulled, the two edges that merge are the same length and your sample will stay flat. For my pattern, the bigger darts are 1½" tall on the selvedge, and the smaller darts are 1" tall. You can use my measurements or vary them if you feel comfortable doing that. Please notice that I included two larger darts and one smaller dart on one-half of the pattern, and four smaller darts on the other half. This will demonstrate two similar but different curves.

Photocopy (or re-draw) this twice so you have two flat copies for later use. Because of the length, you may have to copy each end and tape them together. Of course, you can also simply re-draw the pattern, and that may save paper.

Cut out the triangles from one of the patterns, but don't cut through the left edge; stop about ⅛" short.

Close the top triangle, matching the two long edges, and use a small piece of tape to secure it. Notice that the paper bends but stays flat.

Close the other six triangles with tape. This is your maquette.

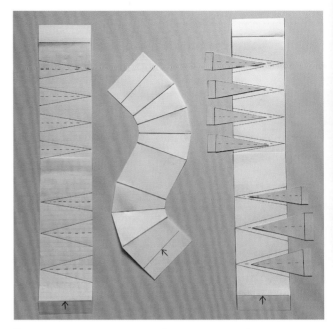

Pattern, maquette, cartoon, and spacers

The cartoon for weaving will be one of the photocopies of the drawn pattern.

You are now ready to start weaving your third sample. Dress your loom or continue on your old warp if there is still enough for this sample. If you are re-dressing your loom, please remember that the warp must be knot-free. My sample is 14½" long woven, and I have 5"–6" of unwoven warp at each end for pulling.

Weave the header to perfectly space the warp, and remember that the header helps you during the pulling process. I like to have at least ½" of header. Follow your cartoon, starting by weaving selvedge to selvedge until you reach the beginning of your first dart.

Once again, you will have to determine how you will weave this particular angle. The first two darts are identical and larger than the remaining five darts. On my sample, I found that this was a sequence of leaving the first two warps on the right unwoven, then a single turn on each of the next three warps, then two unwoven, then a single turn on each of the next three warps, repeat. Remember that you will make your first turn on a valley warp in order to get a smooth angle. For those of you who weave a lot of tapestry, this will come naturally to you. For those of you fairly new to tapestry, this is a good

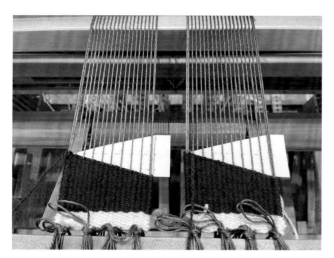

The first dart is woven and the spacer inserted.

The third dart is a lower angle.

lesson. The main thing is to look at what you have woven, and see what looks best.

When you have finished your first angle, insert the spacer, remembering to place it in the last open shed. Wrap the weft around the outside warp on the left once and then continue weaving over the spacer, using the same sequence as in the angle below. If you are on a floor loom, you will beat this section with your fingers or a tapestry fork. As in our previous samples, you will need to push the spacer back into place when needed.

Weave up a few rows, selvedge to selvedge, following your cartoon. Your second dart will be the same as the first, using the same angle sequence. Weave selvedge to selvedge again, and then you will be ready to start your third dart, which is a lower angle than the first two. On my sample I wove from left to right, turning back on each valley warp to achieve this low angle. Insert the spacer. Wrap your weft around the outside warp once and then weave back over your spacer, using the same sequence as below the spacer.

Weave selvedge to selvedge, following your cartoon until you reach the bottom of your fourth dart. These four darts will be woven all the same as the previous dart, except that they are facing the opposite direction.

When you finish the last dart, weave selvedge to selvedge for an inch or more. Weave a header and cut your sample off the loom. Remember that you want 4" or more of unwoven warp, which will help during the

The last four darts will be woven on the opposite side.

pulling process. Tie two or three adjacent warps together in a simple tie if you aren't going to pull the warp immediately. Set your sample on a flat, clean surface until you are ready to pull the warp.

If you want to photocopy this sample, you will probably need to do it in two sections.

Now it is time to plan the sequence for pulling the warp. My sense of logic tells me to start with the side with three darts that were woven first. Starting with the dart closest to the center of the sample, pull the darts consecutively toward you until all three are pulled. Turn the sample around and start with the dart farthest from you, and pull the darts in sequence until all four have been pulled closed.

You have a plan, and it is time to start the pulling process. Get your sample set up on a clean surface. The side with three darts should be closest to you. Leave the header in place. To make these instructions easier, we are going to number the darts. The dart closest to you is 1, the next is 2, and the next is 3. Pull out the spacers from darts 3 and 2. Arrange the tapestry so that the two edges of dart 3, farthest from you, are together. The excess warp from that dart will now be sticking up on top of the tapestry.

You will be using one hand to pull the warp and the other hand to hold the tapestry carefully in place. If you have completed the first two samples, this will feel very natural and will allow you to feel the warp moving inside the warp tunnel. Start from the right side, which has the most open warp. Carefully take hold of the outside double warp in dart 2 and pull that warp until the loop of excess warp disappears from dart 3. Do not overpull! Repeat the pulling sequence across until all the warps from dart 3 have disappeared. As on the previous samples, you may want to use needlenose pliers to grab ahold of the warp threads closest to the point when your fingers won't fit into that space. You may need to go back and gently pull some of the warps if you can still see a bit of the warp showing through. The tapestry should still be flat.

The sample is finished and completed with a header.

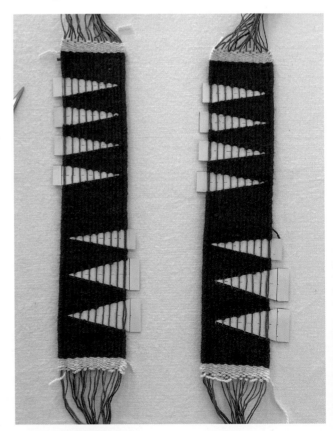

The samples ready to pull

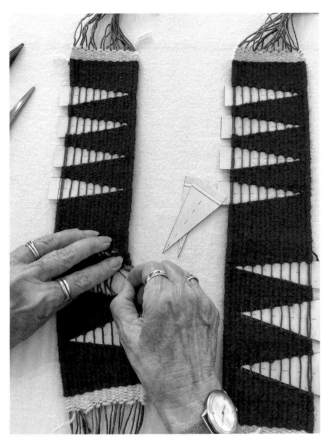

Pull the two sides of the third dart together. Start on the outside edge and pull those warps into the second dart. *Photo by Edward Parsons*

You may need to use needlenose pliers to grasp warp. *Photo by Edward Parsons*

Now arrange the tapestry so that the edges of dart 2 are together. Pull out the spacer from dart 1 and repeat the pulling process until all the warps have been pulled into dart 1. Again, you will need the pliers.

All the warps from the center dart are pulled into the first dart. *Photo by Edward Parsons*

Push the edges of the first dart together and pull all the warps out through the hem edge.

Finally, arrange the tapestry so that the two edges of the front dart are together. Again, the excess warp will loop up on the surface. Pull these warp loops out through the hem edge. The header is still in place and is helping to keep your weft yarns compressed.

Turn the sample around so that the other hem edge is facing you. By now, you should see the logic of this process. Again, we will label these darts, with dart 1 closest to you and dart 4 is the farthest away. You now have the opportunity to tighten the center dart if it needs it. Pull out the spacer from dart 4, and you can gently pull on any warps that are still visible in the middle of dart 3 from the first pull. If that dart looks perfect, you can move on.

Remove the spacer from dart 3 and push together the two edges of dart 4. The excess warp from that dart will now be sticking up on top of the tapestry. Pull the

Your first curve on this sample is complete.

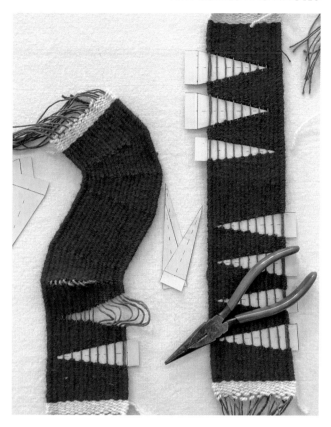

Turn your sample around and, starting with the farthest dart, pull each of them toward you. *Photo by Edward Parsons*

warp from dart 4 into dart 3. Repeat the process of removing a spacer, pushing the edges of a dart together, and pulling that excess warp into the next dart closest to you. Since you are not going to be able to pull any of these darts from both sides, it is important that you complete each pull, making sure you can't see any warps, before you move on to the next dart in the sequence. The final pull will be pulling the warp from dart 1 out through the hem edge toward you. The header stays in place and your sample is flat.

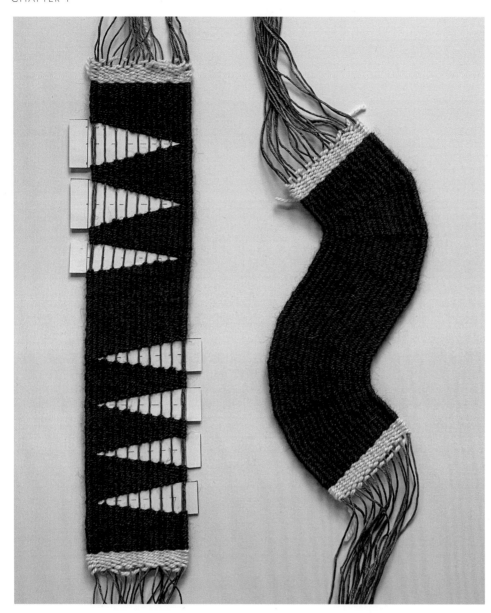

Notice the subtle difference in the two curves.

You have now completed pulling the third sample. Congratulations!

A final thought on flat curves: You may find that it is more logical for you to make cartoons based on previous samples, using the same weft so you know which angles will weave up in the smoothest manner. It depends on what is more important for what you are weaving—the exact curve or the smoothest curve. Sampling is vital to gain this information about each weft yarn.

As you move on to the next chapter about 3-D techniques, keep thinking about these 2-D samples and how you might manipulate them to create dimensional forms.

The sky is the limit with compound curves. Have fun and make a lot of patterns!

Being an artist is a process of finding your visual voice and finding the right tools to bring your ideas to life. There are times when it feels like one long, long series of "What ifs?" When I first discovered weaving, I felt my brain connecting to the tools and materials related to this process in a totally creative way. The ideas poured out of me, and I tried a wide variety of techniques as I searched for something that felt personal and lasting. I had the good luck to discover weaving when I was only 19. I wasn't trying to find a replacement for my love of painting, but weaving seduced me.

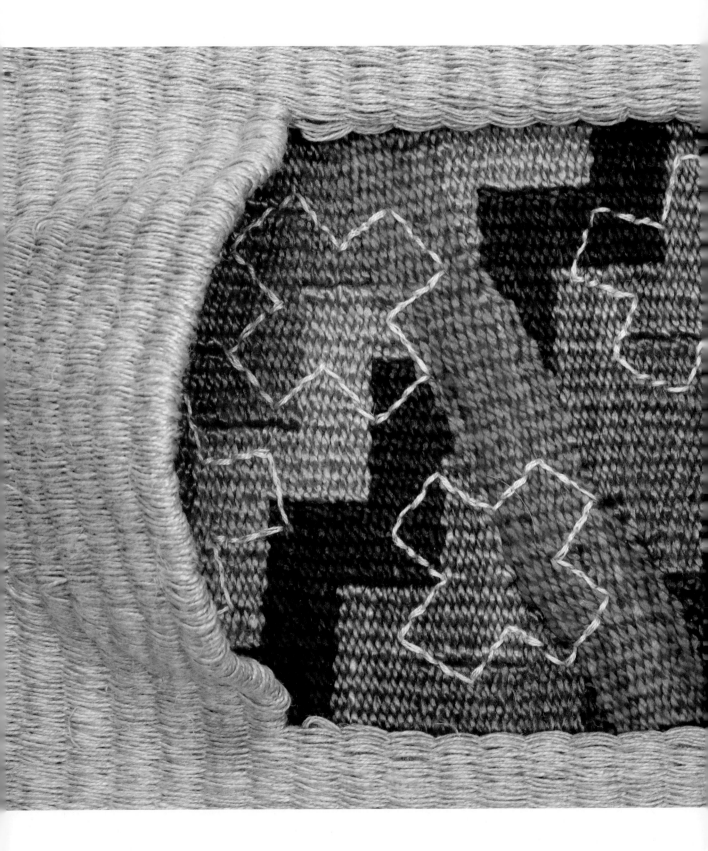

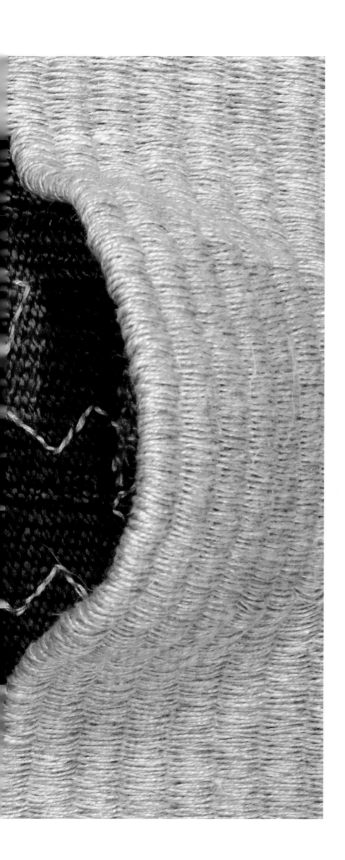

CHAPTER 2

3-D FORMS

In this chapter we will look at some different ways to make tapestry become dimensional. The technical in formation about the pattern-making, weaving, and pulling processes from the first chapter transfers to this section. If you have not woven those samples, I would advise you to go back to that chapter and read it thoroughly to get the basic information before you proceed. I have provided patterns for each of these samples. If you want to try something a little bit different, I recommend that you copy my pattern and make a maquette of it before you design a new pattern and make that maquette. I have not included all the specific steps for weaving that were in the previous chapter, since I am assuming that you understand the need for headings, careful weaving, etc. I have included information that is specific to these samples, and a few reminders about previously covered information.

For the first four samples in this section, you will need a warp that is 6" wide and 3 yards long if you are using a floor loom. Double your selvedge warps. For larger samples, like the first three in this chapter, I seldom weave two identical samples at the same time. Of course, you may choose to put two 6" strips of warp on your loom and weave the pair, one to pull and one to keep as an example. Or you can simply photocopy your sample before you pull it. That, along with your pattern and maquette, should provide you with adequate documentation of the weaving process.

Loops

Loops are strips of weaving that hang off the surface of your tapestry. While this is a very simple sample to weave, it should inspire many possibilities for larger projects.

If you are using a frame loom, set up a warp for a sample that is 6" wide and about 12" long. Remember that you will need 4"–6" of unwoven warp at each end. As with all pulled warp samples, weave a header to space the warps and to hold them in place when the sample is cut off the loom.

The pattern is built of horizontal and vertical

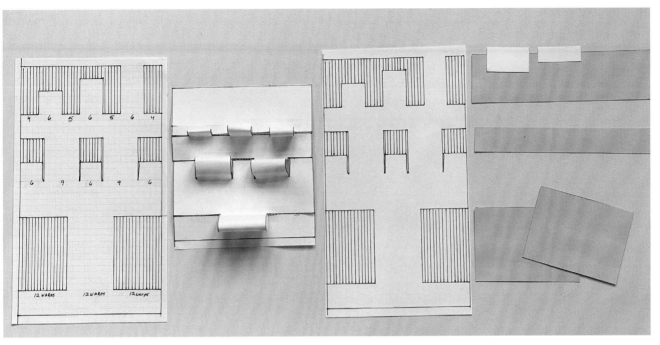

Pattern, maquette, cartoon, and spacers

rectangles. It is easy to get confused with woven and unwoven areas on this pattern, so I included a few lines to represent warps in the areas that will remain unwoven, to remind us where to put the spacers. Please note that the lines on my pattern are not meant to be the number of warps you have in your sample. Look at my pattern and then decide whether you want to copy it or modify it in some small way. I have noted the number of warps in most sections on the pattern. This is important if you want the work to be symmetrical or if you are working with imagery that needs a specific number of warps. For example, if on a project you want centered chevron shapes on one of the loops, you will want an odd number of warps in that section. As before, it is important that you draw out your pattern, make copies, cut and tape one of the copies, so it becomes a maquette for your sample, and then use another copy as the cartoon for weaving.

Because this is all straight weaving with no angles, it is a very quick sample to weave. You will need to carefully watch all the selvedges and keep the warps running perfectly straight. Remember, as with all pulled warp, you need to make sure that the last row you weave before an open warp section and the first row you weave after that section must be in opposite sheds, so that when you pull the warp those two edges will fit together. Note that when weaving the first loop on this sample, I wove from the right selvedge to the left edge of the loop and then continued weaving the loop with the same weft yarn. When the loop was complete, I wove the final row from the right edge of the loop to the left outside selvedge. You can see from the images that the two horizontal edges are in opposite sheds. Depending on the number of loops that you have, you may have to alter this system. Always remember that opposite sheds fit together.

When the first loop is completed, put the spacers in place. Because there are no angles, you do not have to put the spacer in place while you are weaving the loop. This allows you to use the beater on your floor loom for the entire sample.

Weave with a continuous weft

You can use two spacers or one wide one that goes behind the loop.

In the next section, we will weave two shorter loops that will come off the surface and then go flat again after an inch. To achieve this, we will weave short sections between each loop. This means you will be weaving five strips at once, with a lot of selvedges to watch! After 1", I stopped weaving three of the strips and continued weaving the two strips that will become the loops. On my sample I started all the wefts in the same direction, which allows all the spacers to be in the same shed.

The final section has three loops, each of a different length, and like the first loop they will come off the tapestry and go back flat at the same point. A simple way to make the spacers is to cut one large spacer that is 6½"–7" wide that runs all the way across the weaving, and then two smaller spacers that support the shorter loops. I've used different material for the small spacers so you can see what I am describing.

After the spacers go in, you can weave from selvedge to selvedge again for 1½" or 2" and then weave the header.

One long spacer can be used.

You can layer spacers when needed.

The sample is ready to be pulled.

The pull for this sample is fairly straightforward but has some different concerns than for the samples in the previous chapter. The first thing you need to look at is the length of the pulls. Follow each of the open warp sections to see how far you would need to pull them through a woven section. Remember that the farther you need to pull, the more friction there is. I would recommend that you pull the single loop section first. Then turn the sample around and pull the center section. Look carefully at all the open warps in the center section. You will see that some warps can be pulled into the open spaces of the section now closest to you, while some will pull all the way to the hem. On my sample, this means that those few warps that will pull all the way to the hem are traveling through 5½" of woven tapestry. You should pay close attention to those pulls because it will tell you a lot about how far it is possible to pull with the warp sett and weft yarn you used on this sample. After you have pulled the middle section, you can simply pull the final section out through the hem edge.

Now that you have your pulling plan, you can go ahead and start. Keep the tension of each pull consistent. You may want to measure the areas as you go, to help keep the geometry of the sample intact. While this isn't so important on a small sample, it is really important on a larger piece. Stay relaxed and focused.

Fold the loop up and pull the warp out through the hem edge. *Photo by Edward Parsons*

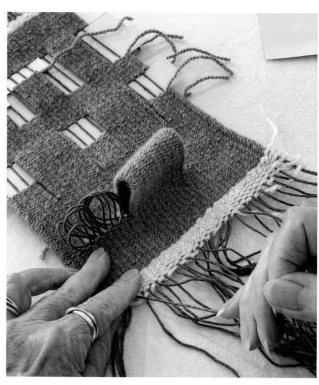

The final few warps get pulled on the first loop. *Photo by Edward Parsons*

Turn your sample and pull the center loop section. *Photo by Edward Parsons*

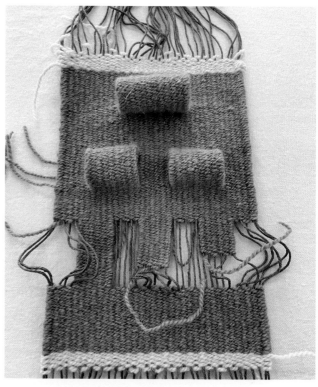

The third section of loops is ready to pull.

The final few warps are pulled. *Photo by Edward Parsons*

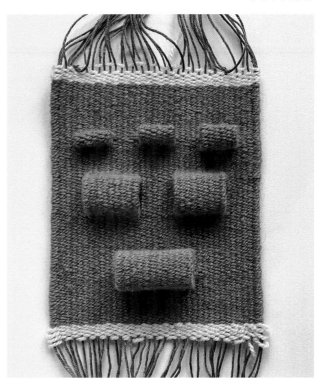

The pulling is complete.

A side view of the completed sample

WHAT IF

What if your loops are dramatically different lengths?

What if you add images to the loops or hide images under the loops?

What if your tapestry has so many loops that you can hardly see the flat areas?

What if you double the warps for the selvedges of all the loops? (Hint: Think about what the surface of the flat areas will look like.)

Flaps and Ridges

Flaps and ridges rise off the surface of the tapestry, or they can be inverted to become recessed areas. Since gravity affects anything coming off the surface, it is important to keep that in mind as you develop your ideas. It is easy to control a ridge if the tapestry will hang so that the ridge is vertical or if the ridge is fairly short (or both). A flap generally is deeper, and gravity will affect it whether it is hung vertically or horizontally. Basically, a ridge becomes a flap when it is long enough to be affected by gravity. Of course, the nature of the materials used will also affect the way a flap hangs.

We will weave three variations of ridges/flaps on this sample. If you are using a frame loom, set up your loom for a sample that will be 6" wide and about 11" long.

I recommend following my pattern or altering it in some small way. You can see that we will be weaving angles again, but this time there is a straight edge at the end of each angle. These spacers are called pickets, and I'm sure you can see why. In this case, the straight section allows the outside edge of the tapestry to remain flat before the ridge or flap rises up off the surface.

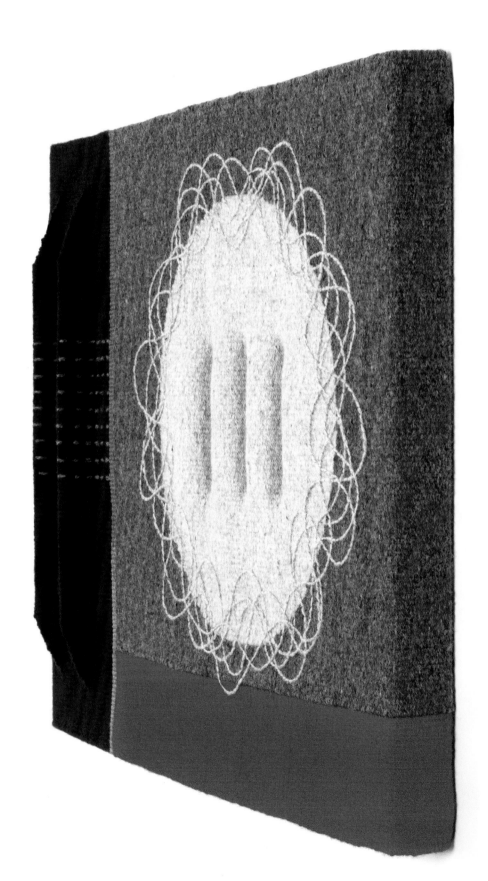

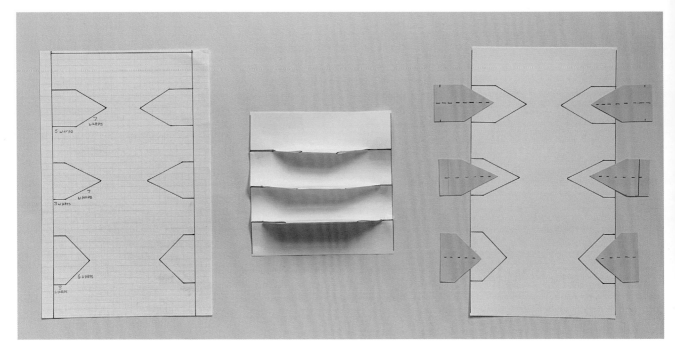

Pattern, maquette, cartoon, and spacers

Make your pattern and maquette.

This sample can be woven with a continuous weft. You should have enough experience to work out the angles. Remember to think about your valleys and hills for smooth angles. As on the curved samples, you will need to put the spacers in place after you have woven the first angle and then beat the weft in by hand as you weave over the top of the spacers. Remember that the spacer may have a tendency to push out the side if you beat too hard. If that happens, push the weft up and push the spacer back into place. Each set of angles on this sample is different.

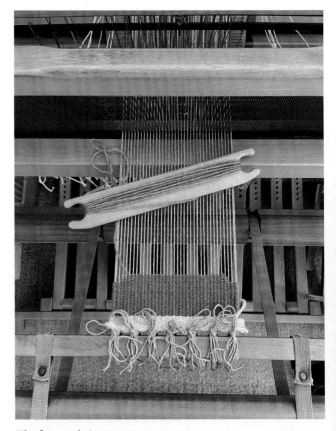

The first angle is woven.

Place the spacers in a shed and weave up, beating by hand.

The first ridge/flap is complete.

Planning the pull is very logical. The center dart should be pulled first into one of the outside darts. The sample then will be turned around, and the center darts can be tightened if necessary. Finally, you will pull the warps of the final darts out through the hem edge.

Please note that for the pull, I have the first ridge we wove farthest away from me as I start the pull. Start with the center darts and pull them into the closest darts, which are the deepest. Pull those end darts out through the hem edge. Of course, the heading and ending are still in place. Turn the sample around and tighten the center dart, starting at the point. It is important to note that the first two warps at the point will have to be tightened from the hem edge, if they need tightening. The remaining center dart warps can be tightened if needed, by pulling gently on the warps in the dart now closest to you, which is the tallest. After you are happy with the center dart, pull the warps from the final dart out through the hem edge.

The weaving is complete.

The sample is ready to pull.

The center pickets can be pulled into the picket closest to you. *Photo by Edward Parsons*

The center two warps of the center ridge on each side need to be pulled through to the hem edge. *Photo by Edward Parsons*

The remaining warps can be pulled into the first picket space. *Photo by Edward Parsons*

The first two ridges are complete.

Turn the sample around and pull the final ridge/flap out through the hem edge.

This sample is now complete. You have probably noticed that there is a lot of energy in the ridges and flaps. Depending on your yarns and how firmly you beat the tapestry, the fabric will be more or less boardy. This sample and others will help you determine how deep your ridges and flaps will need to be for your purposes.

You can see that the tallest picket makes a ridge that can be bent over to be a flap.

You may want to gently rotate the fabric by the edge of a pull to redistribute the weft yarns. This can make the pull line smoother and less visible. *Photo by Edward Parsons*

In some cases you may need to manipulate the pulled area with your hands to distribute the weft yarns more evenly. Don't be afraid to push the ridges in and out or rotate the fabric a bit. Remember that a flap on the surface can become a recessed area by simply pushing it out the back of the tapestry.

Look at your sample in both the horizontal and vertical positions.

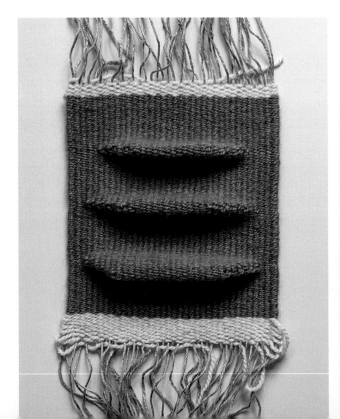

What if you weave a sample using a softer warp such as 3/2 perle cotton?

What if your angle for the ridge or flap started at the selvedge edge, so your spacer would be a dart, not a picket?

What if you place several ridges very close together?

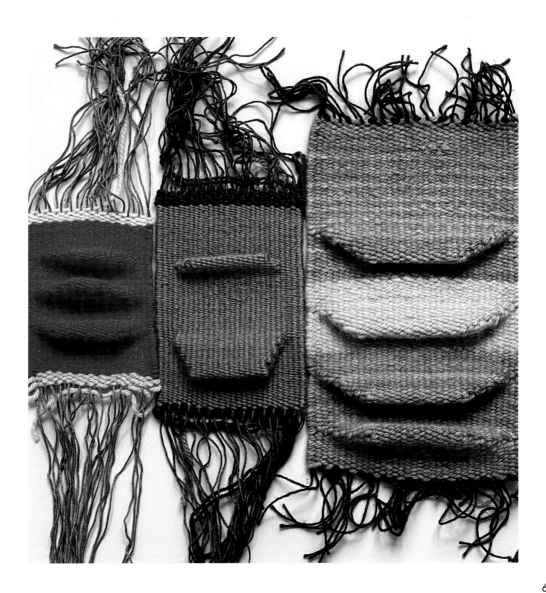

Ripples

Ripples are used to make the tapestry undulate, and can look like ruffles or soft folds in the fabric. They can be placed at either selvedge of the tapestry, or they can be put—with a little more complexity—into the body of a tapestry. There are two samples in this section. The first sample covers the basics, and the second is a variation of a ripple within the body of a tapestry.

I would strongly recommend following my patterns for these samples. As in the previous sample, our primary spacer will be a picket. The first ripple will be on the selvedge. For the second ripple there is a slit next to it that is twice the width of the picket, and a woven rectangle between the picket and the selvedge that is the same width as the picket. This allows the tapestry to lie flat around the ripple. As on all these samples, draw your pattern, copy it twice, cut and tape one of the copies for your maquette, and use one for your cartoon.

Re-tension your floor loom or set up your frame loom for the first sample, which is 6" wide and 9" long. Weave in the header. Follow your cartoon carefully as you weave, being very careful with the placement of your slit. If you have already completed the previous samples, this will be quite easy.

Planning the pull should also make sense to you now. It really doesn't matter which of the ripples you pull first, but look carefully at each section so you know where you want to start and to end. I have chosen to first pull the side with the ripple that will be surrounded by flat tapestry, and then pull the side with the single picket.

Pull out both the short picket and the rectangle spacer. Pull the two edges of the rectangle together and, starting from the outside edge, pull the warps through to the hem edge. Next, pull a few of the warps on the other selvedge. Because this picket is fairly long, I would next recommend pulling a few warps in the center of the

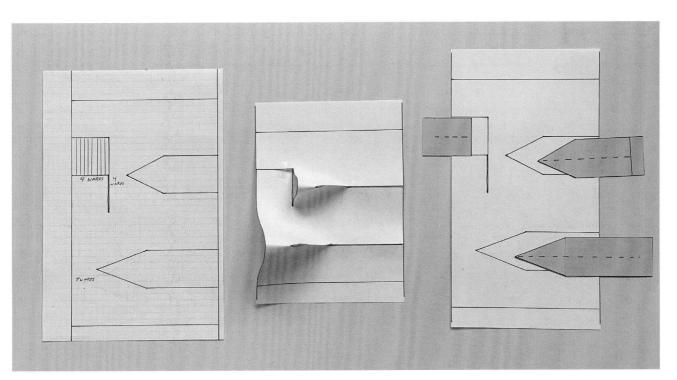

Pattern, maquette, cartoon, and spacers

The first sample on the loom completed

The sample is ready to pull.

picket. This will help hold the two edges together as you pull the remaining warps. Remember that it is better to pull firmly but gently the first time across and then go back and pull a second time if needed.

Turn the sample around and remove the single picket. Check to see if you need to tighten any warps from the section you just pulled before you pull this picket closed. This pull will be done in the same manner as the last one. Start pulling from the selvedge and then pull a few warps in the middle before pulling all the warps out through the hem edge. You should now have two lovely ripples coming off the surface of your sample. Congratulations!

Start on the right side and pull the warp from the rectangular spacer. *Photo by Edward Parsons*

Pull a few warps on the outside edge and then some in the center.

The first ripple is pulled and the sample is turned around.

Pull the second ripple. *Photo by Edward Parsons*

The sample is pulled with a photocopy of the unpulled sample.

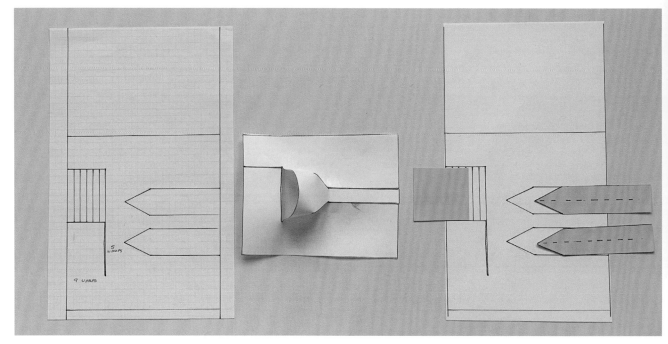

Pattern, maquette, cartoon, and spacers

The second sample has a ripple with more volume, due to two darts above the slit and lower band of weaving. Since this is a variation of the previous sample, weaving it is certainly optional, but how can you resist not weaving it? If you decide not to weave this sample, I would still encourage you to make the pattern and the maquette. It is 6" wide and 7" long. Follow the instructions of the previous sample.

For this pull, I chose to pull one of the pickets first, and then I pulled the remaining picket and the square space at the same time. This order fits my logic but is just a suggestion.

The sample is woven and ready to pull.

Pulling the first picket. *Photo by Edward Parsons*

Turn the sample and prepare for pull.

Pull the picket, starting with the outside edge and then a few warps in the center. *Photo by Edward Parsons*

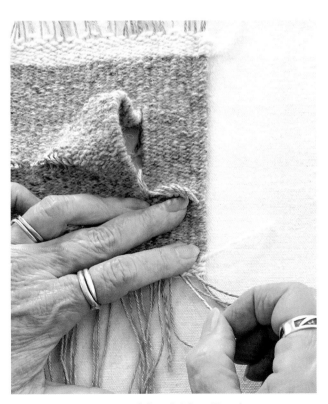

Pull the square section and then finish pulling the picket. *Photo by Edward Parsons*

The finished sample and photocopy of unpulled sample

When I give workshops on pulled warp, I show a completed pulled sample of the ripple surrounded by flat tapestry, and ask the students to figure out the cartoon for it. For many students, this can be quite difficult and sometimes frustrating. This exercise really demonstrates how aspects of pulled warp can be counterintuitive. It also shows how important making the maquette really is when you want a successful sample.

I have woven quite a few tapestries with ripples, and each one teaches me something new. Making a maquette of your pattern should never be deleted from your process. On large pieces, I will sometimes turn the full-scale pattern into the maquette and then simply flatten it out again and tape new paper into the cut-out spacer sections. This saves time and paper while still making sure that the form I want is the form I will get. I also save all my patterns so they can be reused or modified.

What if the ripples are close, mirror imaged so that they are on both selvedges, and the fabric is narrow?

What if the ripples vary in size?

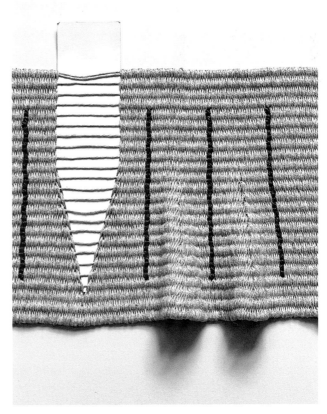

Curves That Aren't Flat

3-D CURVE

This sample is similar to the very first curved sample, except that the darts do not go from selvedge to selvedge. This will cause a lip to form along one edge of the curve. You have all the basic technical information to weave this sample. The woven length is about 10", and it is 3" wide. Since you have woven other samples using darts, I have not included step-by-step written instructions here. The images below will give you all the information you need to complete this simple sample.

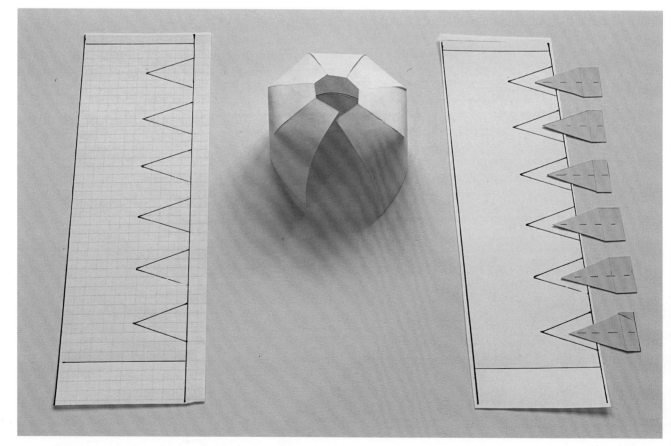

Pattern, maquette, cartoon, and spacers

Start from the center and work toward each hem edge.
Photo by Edward Parsons

You will see the form emerging early in the process.
Photo by Edward Parsons

You may need to turn or rotate the sample for ease in
pulling the warp. *Photo by Edward Parsons*

Pull the final warps out through the hem edge. *Photo by
Edward Parsons*

The finished sample and photocopy of unpulled sample

Note about the yarns: For this sample I used a hand-painted, variegated wool yarn for the sample to be pulled, and natural wool for the control sample.

What if you put some darts on one selvedge and some on the other?

What if the darts are different widths or lengths?

What if you want to make a sphere? Yes, that is possible, just not easy—and no, I have not tried to make one. I know the limits of my patience.

SPIRAL

A spiral shape can be woven using the same basic method as the first flat, curved sample. You will need to increase the number of darts and make them very close together. I bet you thought about a spiral shape as you were making that very first curved pattern. It does, however, take a great deal of weaving and a lot of darts to get a satisfying spiral form.

Hint: It is a good or reasonable idea to make your darts a size that is easy to weave. To do this, weave a couple of test angles with the yarn you want to use for this sample. Then use that angle to determine the shape of your darts on your pattern/model. Remember that small darts make a smoother curve.

Decide how wide of a strip you want to weave, and cut two strips of graph paper to that width. You will use one strip for the model and one strip for the pattern. They should be identical. The strips will have to be fairly long to really make a spiral, so tape additional strips together and then start drawing out your triangles for the darts. Remember to make the center line of each

Nicki Bair. *My Tapestry Spiral*, 2009, variable size. Tapestry, 13 yards long and 4" wide when woven, 182 darts. *Courtesy of Nicki Bair*

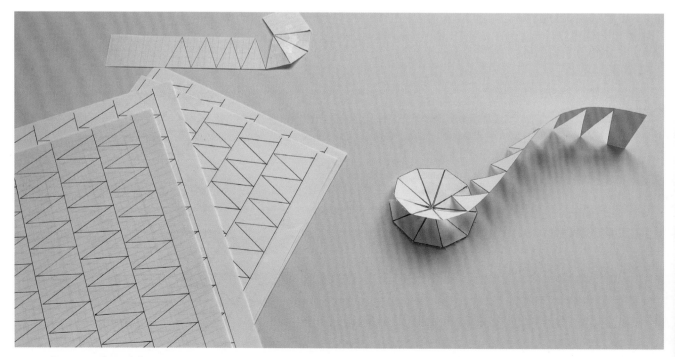

Pattern and partial maquette

The narrow warp is tied on to a simple frame loom with extra warp at the top.

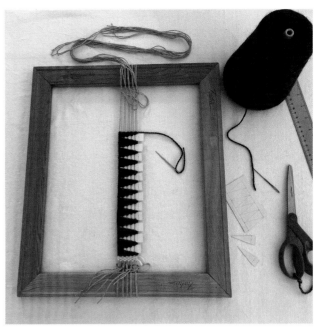

Weave up to near the top of your loom.

dart perpendicular to the warp, and the two sides of the triangle the same length. Review the directions for the first sample if necessary. After you have drawn out several darts, cut them out on the strip you will use for a model, and tape them closed to make sure that you are actually making a spiral. It may be surprising to find out how many darts you will need to make a spiral. The darts will also need to be close to each other. Continue making your model and pattern, adding additional paper as needed. You can measure the outside edge of your maquette once you have completed one circle, then multiply it by the number of spirals you want. This will determine the length you will need for your warp.

Shortcut: This works if all your darts will be the same size and spaced the same throughout the spiral. After you determine the size of your darts, draw them out on one sheet of paper and photocopy it multiple times so you can use these strips to build both your pattern and your model.

Dress your loom to the required width with a warp long enough to accommodate your pattern. We doubled the outside warps on the first samples, but you may want to use a single warp at the selvedge if you did not like the heavier edge of the early samples. It might be interesting to double the warp on the outside selvedge but not on the selvedge with the darts, which is the inside edge of the spiral.

Even if you are using a tall frame loom, it may not be large enough for a good spiral. You can dress your frame loom by tying on your warp so that there is extra warp at the top of the frame. After you weave up to the top of the loom, untie the warp from the top, wrap the woven spiral around the bottom bar of your loom, and re-tie the warp to the top bar. You can see from the images that I added an extra board to the bottom bar of my frame before I wound the tapestry around it. It is held in place with loop-and-hook fasteners. Or, you can just build a very tall frame loom or use a simple backstrap loom for this sample. Weavers are very inventive; you will find a way to weave this.

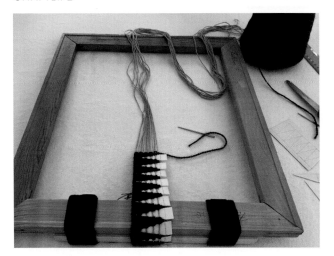

The warp has been untied from the top, and the tapestry wound around the bottom of the frame. Note the extra board attached to the frame.

The warp is re-tensioned at the top, and weaving continues.

You can weave this just as you did the first flat, curved sample.

The pull for the spiral should start in the center, and then you can work toward each end. You may need the needlenose pliers to pull the warps near the point of each dart. This pull will get messy because of the length of warp you will be pulling. Keep your warps as organized as possible. Be very patient. This is a process that can seem to get totally out of control before it is over.

WHAT IF

What if the spiral changes width by periodically adding or dropping warps?

What if after a couple of spirals the darts are moved to the other selvedge?

What if you use progressions of different-sized darts, from very low angles to 90-degree angles?

Organic Surfaces

This is a very flexible and experimental sample, and I suggest that you play with several patterns before you decide what to do. Some of your spacers may be quite irregular. In some cases you may need to make your maquette out of fabric or interfacing because the paper may be too stiff to manipulate. I recommend that you try a lot of different open spaces and simply play with this sample.

You will very likely find that this sample, or completed work done with this technique, will need a backing of some sort or require some stitching to stabilize the form. You can easily stitch the flat sections of the tapestry to the backing to hold them in place. You can also add stuffing to maintain the 3-D sections. This isn't cheating, it is being inventive.

A few years ago I wove a small dimensional sample that has flattened out completely so that the outside edge became irregular. There were several reasons for this. First, I did not back it to anything that would have maintained the exterior rectangular shape. It was woven with silk weft, which seemed to slide around and flatten.

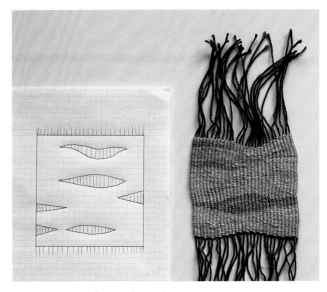

The pattern and flattened sample

It was designed to have subtle undulations on the surface, so the dimensionality was limited to start with. The final problem was that I packed it in a suitcase for workshops one too many times. You can see in the images that when I pin it into a rectangular shape, the undulations appear. For this I was working on a fabric-covered 3" foam form.

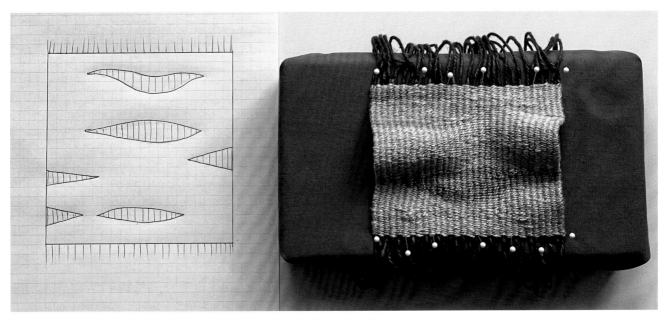

The sample pinned into a rectangular shape to become dimensional

What to Think About Now That You Have Completed All the Samples

I hope that you have learned so much from these samples that you are teeming with new ideas for your tapestries. Remember that I did quite a bit of technical work with this technique before I had a good reason to apply it to

my own work. Your own applications may take time to emerge. Be patient. I do hope that you find a reason to use pulled warp in the very near future.

Capturing Your Ideas

Pulled warp, by itself, is not a concept for your work, but it is a technique that can facilitate the formation of ideas as you investigate the technical possibilities. Creative thinking about one thing frequently opens other doors for more creativity. Keep your sketchbook handy. When some "What if" idea pops into your mind as you are working on your samples, draw a quick thumbnail sketch. Don't wait until later to do the sketch. Don't try to think it through. Simply get something down on paper so you can look back at it later. Then develop this kernel of an idea with additional thumbnail sketches. It just might turn into an idea that needs to be woven.

Everyone finds their own path to idea formation. There is no simple rule for this. Keep your mind open, listen to your intuition, look at everything, and draw a lot. Ask yourself some questions about what really matters to you. The idea/concept that you work with for a year or a lifetime of work can be simple, extremely complex, or something in between. It does not necessarily need to please others, but it should be visually interesting, ask more questions than it answers, and engage a viewer for a period of time. And most of all, it must be deeply important to you.

About Drawing

Drawing is simply eye/hand coordination, and I believe that everyone with a studio practice should learn to draw well enough to get an idea or a composition down on paper quickly and fairly accurately. It doesn't need to be a beautiful drawing. Even if you work primarily with photographic images for your source material, being able to explore how you will use or alter that information is very helpful. You don't need to share these drawings with anyone else unless you choose to do so. They are visual clues that will help you sort out your thinking process. They work well together with collages, photos, and other source material as you determine which ideas need to be made tangible.

Magenta Morning (side view), 2022. Tapestry, wool and silk on linen
warp: 10.5" × 10.5" × 3". *Photo by Taylor Dabney*

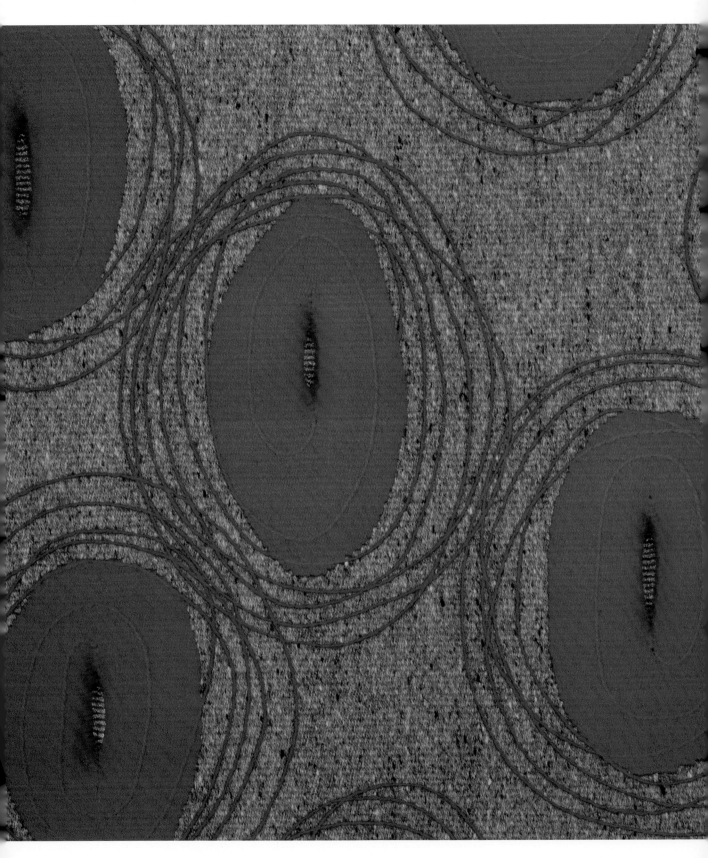

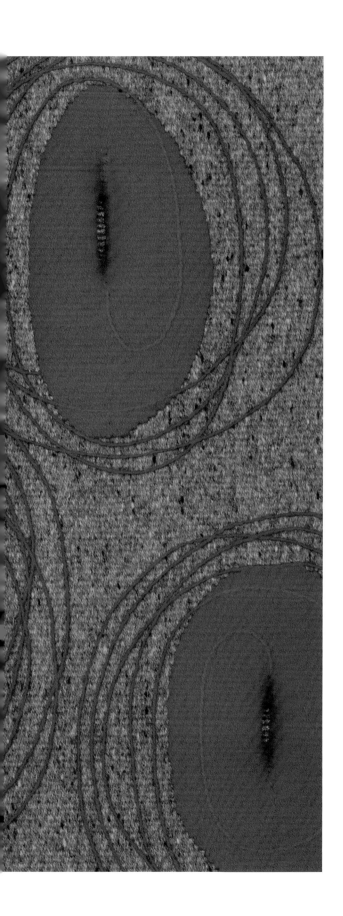

CHAPTER 3

COMPLEX PULLS

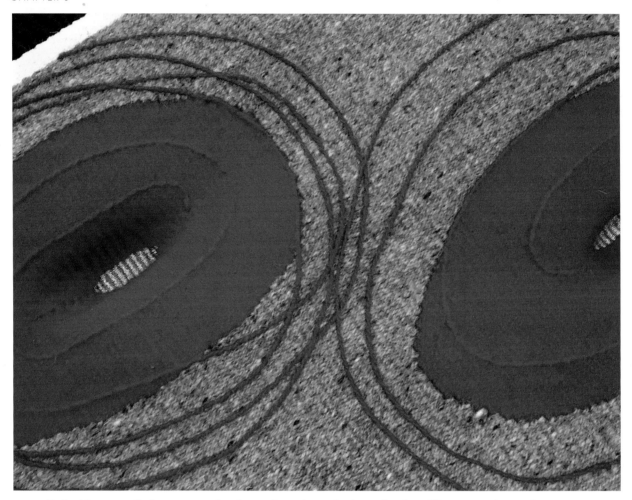

Embroidery on pulled warp tapestries almost always has to be done after the pulling process is complete.

The samples you have woven so far have taught you a great deal about the basics of pulled warp. You now should have gained a good understanding of the need to plan out the order of each pull. You will run into different challenges when you apply this technique to larger or more-complex tapestries.

What makes a pull complex? The two things that I have found that make the pulling process more difficult are the overall size of the tapestry and the need to pull through image areas that have a lot of color changes. For the most part, your biggest technical challenge will be in making sure that you have access to the warps that you need to pull, where you need to pull them.

To make these decisions, you should have a good understanding of the materials that you are using for both warp and weft. Always keep in mind that the level of friction between the warp and weft along with the length of the pull will determine the ease of the pull. For those of you who are adventurous with the yarns you weave with, this may be your primary concern. This is true especially if you have some areas with low-friction fibers such as cotton and some with high-friction materials such as goat hair or a fuzzy wool. If you are weaving an elaborate image and you will have to pull warp through that area, be very careful. Keep your weft even and do not allow the warp to pull in or push out. I do not recommend using eccentric weft for pulled warp. I'm not saying that it is impossible to pull warp through an area of eccentric weft, but it is difficult, since the warps will automatically try to move when the tapestry comes off the

Pulse as it was being woven

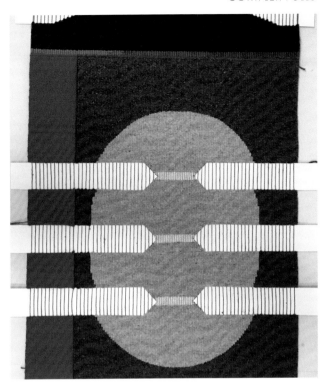

Pulse flat on my work table

loom. Remember that a small sample can save you time and grief in the long run.

Have I ever scrapped an idea because I found that what I wanted was not possible? Yes. Have I ever modified an idea to make it technically possible? Sure. Have I ever compromised aesthetics in order to do this? I hope not. Pulled warp opens a lot of options for 3-D and curved tapestries, but it is not a solution for every idea.

How you approach idea development in your studio practice is up to you. Everyone has a different level of exploration in the development of their work, a level of spontaneity, a set of rules, or something else that controls the process. It is imperative that if you want a specific end result with pulled warp, you must think it all the way through to the final finishing before you start. It has to be not just a good idea, but also a workable idea. I am sharing some of the aspects of several more-complex pulls to add to your knowledge base. These may not be the exact problems you will encounter, but they should help you understand some common technical issues so that you are able to solve related problems.

Sometimes an idea for a pulled warp tapestry can seem very easy, and you might be inclined to skip planning out the pull before you start weaving. Do not skip this vital step in the process. My tapestry *Pulse* is a case in point. It has five ridges, two coming off the surface and three inverted. At first glance, it looks as if the two black ridges on the left side will pull easily out of that side, and the three inverted ridges will pull out of the other side. The tapestry is only 31½" wide. It was designed to be mounted on a support frame that is 2" deep to accommodate the depth of the inverted ridges. That means that the tapestry needs to be almost 4" wider on each side than the image, so that it can fold around the frame and be attached to the back. Through experience, I had found that with these yarns, I could easily pull the warp through 6–10" of woven tapestry. When I measured the length of the tapestry that I would need to pull through, it was between 12 and 13". Too long for an easy pull. I had to make a decision about taking a chance that it would be difficult but possible, or add an extra spacer to keep the pull at 8". I made the reasonable decision to

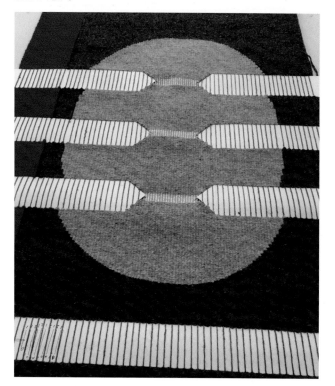

Ready to pull the warp for the three ridges

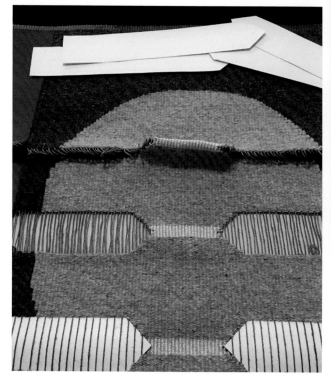

First spacers pulled out

add the spacer. Although it added an additional pull and additional time, it worked well and was the right decision.

Adding an additional spacer that goes all the way across the warp gives you access to the warp you need to pull, where you need it. When you do this, you will then need to pull all the warps from this section during the next pull. In the case of *Pulse*, the next pull would be out of the warp end, so that was not a problem. Just be advised that every change you make may alter the next step. You don't want to add pulls that aren't really necessary.

Pulse is also a good example of how odd an image might look when it is separated by spacers. The circle looks as if it will not be a circle, and yet, after the pulling is complete, it is as perfect as I can weave a circle. You have to have faith in the cartoon you prepared and follow it exactly in situations like this. For pulled warp with images, the image can be drawn directly onto the maquette. Then the maquette can be flattened to become

the tapestry cartoon. That is the way I generally approach this issue.

Note that the pulling process is always done with the front of the tapestry facing up. The ridges that will become inverted are simply pushed in when the tapestry is mounted.

One of my most difficult pull sequences involved *Before the Stars*. This tapestry, 24.75" × 45.5" × 2", has six inverted ridges scattered over a wide area. In order to really understand the pulling sequence, it is necessary to follow each warp that needs to be pulled to the area where it needs to end up. You cannot pull over three-dimensional shapes. You can pull only on a flat surface. This means that you can't always pull every warp from one spacer into the next and then move on to the following spacer.

My original plan was to pull all the warp in one direction. Look at the image of the tapestry, draped over the work table. For sake of clarity, we will label the rows of spacers as 1 through 7, with 7 being closest to the front warp edge.

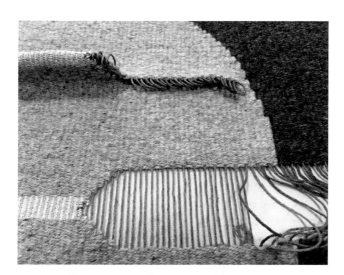

Pulling progresses from right to left.

Final ridge pulled into extra selvedge-to-selvedge spacer.

I first pulled most of the warp from the 1st spacer into the 2nd spacer. A small ridge formed on the right side, and all the warps pulled easily except for the warps that were directly above the ridge on the left side of the 2nd spacer. Those warps would be pulled next into spacer rows 3/4 before I pulled the remaining warp from row 2 into the 3rd/4th row. This row includes a pair of spacers that form the inverted ridge, and then a straight spacer that goes from selvedge to selvedge. My decision to add this extra spacer was determined by measuring the length of woven fabric that the warp must be pulled

Before the Stars is laid out on the work table.

through. From experience I knew that the warp would quite nicely pull through 10" or 12" of tapestry woven with these yarns. If I hadn't added that extra spacer, the warps that passed through the small gold area would have had to be pulled 18".

In hindsight, I should have also added additional selvedge-to-selvedge spacers to rows 5, 6, and 7. All these pulls exceeded my decision to pull 12" or less. These other pulls all were 12" to 17" and were successful, but they were not easy. I clearly remember thinking that I may have made a real mistake as I started each of the long areas of the pull. These sections were small, involving only 11 warps. The problem was that there was so much friction due to the length of the pull that I had to exert a lot of controlled effort at the beginning of the pull, then almost immediately dial that back once the warp started to move.

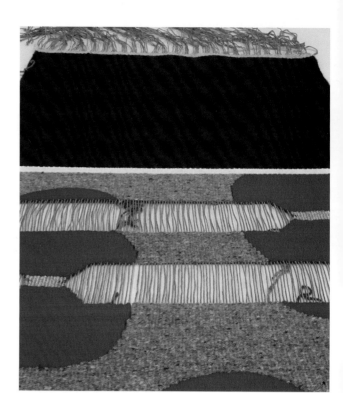

The first two rows of spacers are removed.

The warp in the 1st spacer is on the surface, and the pulling has begun on the right side.

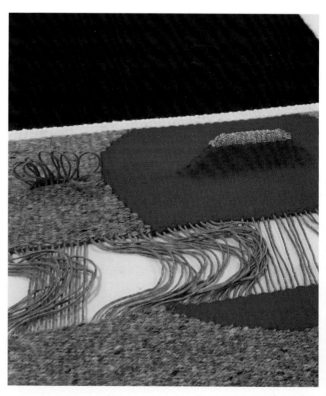

The pulling progresses.

This pull was also slightly more difficult because of the number of spacers. As I pulled toward myself, the length of each warp got longer and longer. That just meant that I had to spend a fair amount of time organizing the warps to keep them from tangling. Every time I pulled a warp, I very carefully moved it off to the side. It is important that you don't accidentally pull on a warp that has already been pulled. It is difficult to ease the warp back into place once you have overpulled.

The remaining warps on the left side, from the 1st spacer, will now need to be pulled all the way to spacers 3 and 4.

Careful pulling to keep everything straight. The small section of warp on top of the gray area, toward the back, will need to be pulled through the gold and pink section where spacer 3 was into spacer row 4.

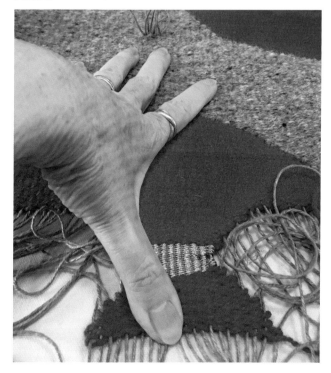

Pulling that small section of gray through the center of a ridge. *Photo by Edward Parsons*

Twilight's Passing has a simple composition with three long loops that overhang each other. The pattern was simple, the weaving was easy, and the pull was not really complex. It did, however, have a difficulty factor since its straightforward composition was dependent on precision. The images here show how carefully I needed to pull to keep the tapestry straight, and how orderly the warps needed to be kept so that I didn't create a tangled mess. I measured each section on both sides frequently to verify that I wasn't overpulling or under-pulling an area. Even when you are being careful, it is difficult to pull each warp identically.

The V-shaped tapestries I wove in the '70s had one large dart in the center. I don't have decent process images from that time period, but if you look at the drawing, you can see that I needed to add selvedge-to-sel-vedge spacers throughout the entire tapestry. This allowed me to make pulls of a reasonable length but added to the problem of keeping the legs of the V as straight as possible. I had to pull carefully and check the straightness of the outside edges on a regular basis. While I had to have 12 selvedge-to-selvedge spacers, I

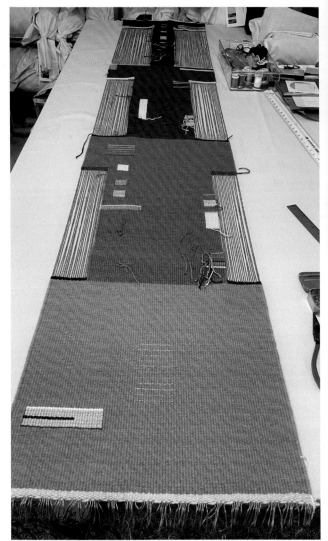

Twilight's Passing before the pulling process is 8' long.

Most of the tapestry is rolled around a foam tube as I start to pull the warps.

The warps are kept as orderly as possible during the pulling process. *Photo by Edward Parsons*

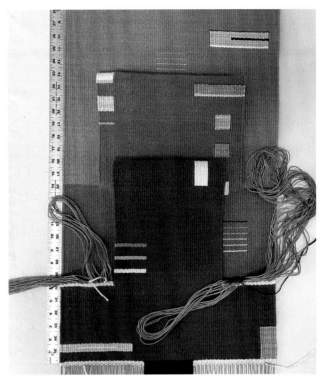

I kept a yardstick next to the tapestry's selvedge to ensure that it stayed straight.

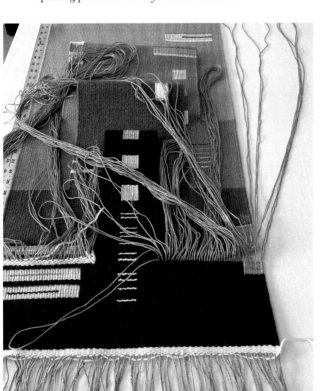

Keeping the warp organized became more difficult by the time I pulled the final section.

The tapestry has been turned, and you can see how much warp was pulled through the tapestry.

Twilight's Passing, 2022.
Tapestry, wool and silk on
linen warp: 30" × 18" × 5".
Photo by Taylor Dabney

did not have to use spacers to support the actual angle of the dart. When an angle is that steep, it is self-supporting.

Getting the results you want with pulled warp may take extra planning time. If you weave samples and if you think carefully about each step, almost anything is possible. Remember that sometimes the pulled warp process does seem to be counterintuitive. When in doubt, stop, analyze the problem, and then carefully resume the planning of something new and wonderful.

Weaving a sample has never been a waste of time for me. I have learned what I want to do, and, even more importantly, I have learned what I don't want to do.

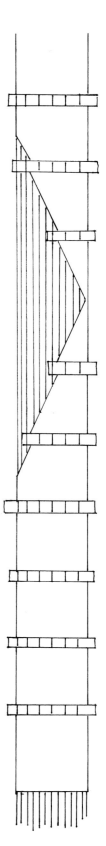

The V-shaped tapestries required multiple selvedge-to-selvedge spacers.

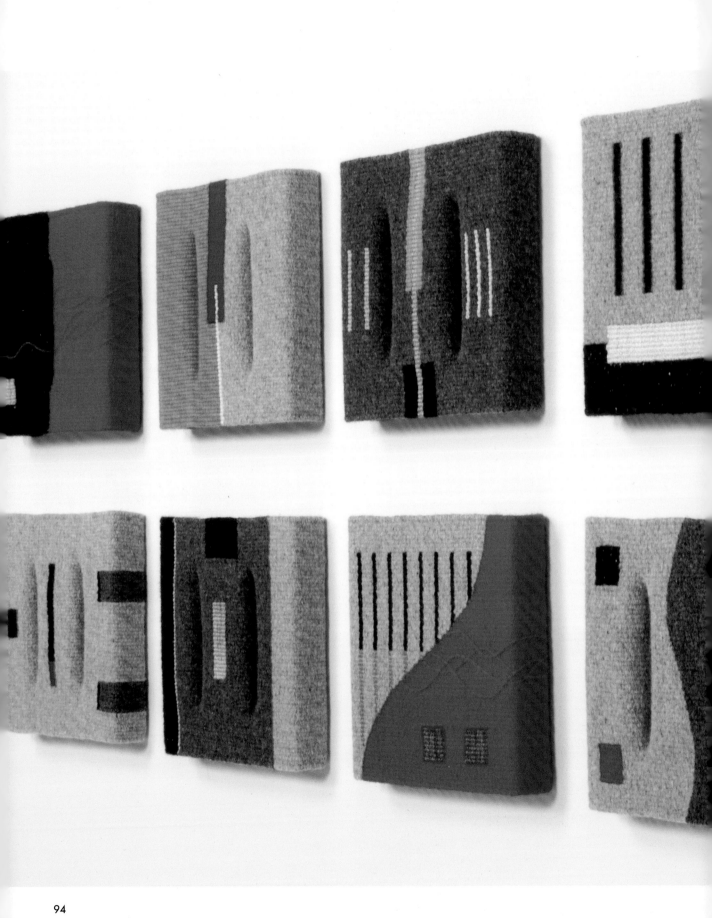

94

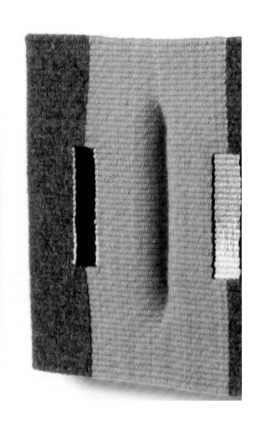

CHAPTER 4

FINISHING SOLUTIONS

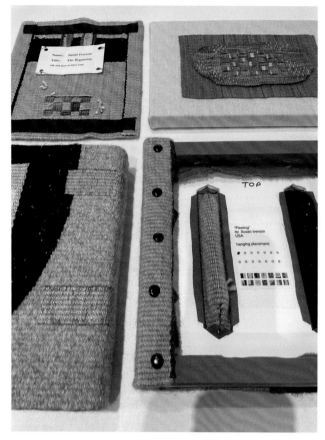

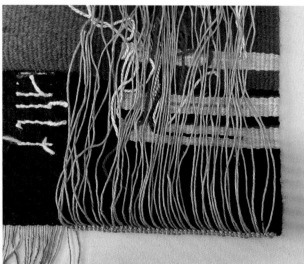

Variation of a Damascus edge on *Twilight's Passing*

The finishing of a pulled warp tapestry can sometimes be as simple as that of a flat tapestry. There are other times when the finishing may be more complicated. As with the pulling process, finishing issues should be considered before you start weaving. Most of the finishing will need to be done after you have completed the pulling process.

Basically, you need to stabilize the tapestry, protect it, and present it in a professional manner. There are many different ways to do this. The majority of my tapestries simply hang on the wall from hook-and-loop fastener strips.

Warp Ends

Warp ends need to be stabilized, and most weavers have a couple of favorite techniques to accomplish this. If you don't have a lot of finishing experience, please refer to a general tapestry book such as *The Art of Tapestry Weaving* by Rebecca Mezoff. There are so many different knots and braids to choose from that you will want to try several until you find one that meets your physical and aesthetic needs. I generally use a variation of the Half Damascus edge on most of my hem edges. This variation is illustrated in fig. 382d in *The Techniques of Rug Weaving* by Peter Collingwood and should be done from the back of the tapestry. After completing the warp edge, I tack the warp ends down with sewing thread and then cut them to about 1". If you like the way that looks, you can stop at that point. I frequently fold 1½" of the tapestry under and hand-stitch it down to make a hem.

On very small tapestries or on curved edges, I use two slightly different techniques to stabilize the warp. They both start with using a doubled sewing thread to run up and down along with the warp. If the tapestry is to be mounted or framed, I sew in only one direction. If the edge is going to hang or if it will come off the surface, I sew across the edge in one direction and then turn back in the other direction so that the thread is making a figure eight shape. This makes the edge more secure. These techniques should be done from the back of the tapestry.

After the warp edge is stable, I have two choices. One is to finger-press the warps onto the back of the tapestry and stitch them down. That works if the back of the tapestry will not be visible. If the back will be visible, then I simply and carefully cut the warps off. I have done this only on small works where there will be no stress placed on that edge. This would be a wonderful finishing technique to try on one of your samples.

The doubled thread is knotted to the back, then the thread travels down the outside warp and then up the second warp.

The thread progresses up one warp and down the next all the way across.

The warp edge is secured with the thread. Note you can see small loops of thread because of color contrast.

The warp ends are finger-pressed away from the warp edge and stitched down.

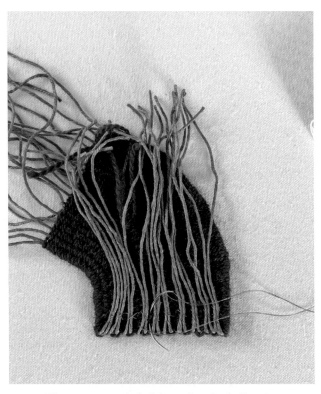

The warps are stitched down from both directions.

Cut all the warp ends off to about 1".

Again, sew up and down each warp with a doubled thread.

Note that the sewing thread is invisible if it is the same color as the weft.

Carefully cut off each warp as short as possible.

The back is now finished.

The front of the sample

You may also want to consider the Swedish edge, which involves working the warp ends, or at least half of them, back into the body of the tapestry. You will need to weave with additional weft in the hem area to accommodate the addition of these U-turned warps. This technique is clearly diagramed in the Peter Collingwood book. It is worth exploring.

Weft Ends

I do believe that the back of a tapestry is like the back of anything and generally is not finished to the same degree as the front. If the back of the tapestry will not be seen, I simply cut off the excess weft ends to about ½". If there are any weft ends close to the selvedges, I weave them back in by running them along with a warp, or I sew them down so that they can't be visible from the side.

When the back of a tapestry will be seen, the weft ends need to be invisible. I weave all the weft ends back into the tapestry. There are several other different ways to finish your weft ends, and the Mezoff book has very good images and explanations of these techniques.

Weft ends on the back of the tapestry may be secured by running them along with a warp. The remaining weft tail can be cut off flush with the tapestry if the back will be visible.

Putting Your Tapestry on the Wall

The majority of my tapestries simply hang from hook-and-loop fasteners. The soft side (loop) of the fastener is machine-sewn onto a cotton tape that is then hand-sewn onto the top edge of the back of the tapestry. The hard side of the fastener is stapled directly onto the wall or adhered to boards that are attached to the wall or hung from a cable-and-hook system. The tapestry can then be easily pressed into place. The staples leave very small holes in the wall and can be quickly filled with spackling compound when the tapestry is moved.

Mounting a Tapestry

There are times when you will want to mount a tapestry on a frame or panel for easy hanging or to give it more support. I do sometimes like the additional physical presence that a 1"–2" deep mount can give to a tapestry. In the case of my tapestries that have inverted ridges, I have to provide a physical space for those ridges, and a mount does that.

Fleeting, a piece composed of 14 small panels, required mounts that could accommodate inverted ridges. I had hoped to use pre-stretched canvases for this, but when I tried to mount the first one, I realized that the canvas was not supportive enough for the panels that had two inverted ridges. I regrouped and had custom frames made by a local woodworker, then mounted acid-free foam core board onto the surface. The foam core board was cut to accommodate the inverted ridges. Fabric was then stretched over the frame and cut so that it could be turned over the edges of the openings and held down with acid-free, double-sided tape. I used a product that prevented fraying before I cut the fabric. I also added a small piece of the hook side of a hook-and-loop fastener (clothing quality) along the top edge of the front of the mount. When I placed my tapestry on the mount, this held the top edge in place without requiring stitching.

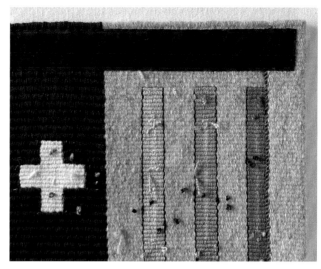

Strip of loop fastener machine stitched onto a twill tape and then hand-stitched to the back of a tapestry

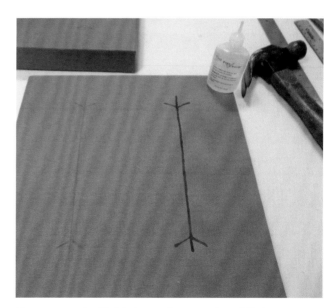

Frame covered with fabric over foam core board that has been cut to accommodate inverted ridges. Lines to be cut are treated with a product that will prevent fraying.

The tapestry panels were simply secured to the back of the frame with upholstery tacks. This whole process was time consuming, but the end result was just right for what I needed.

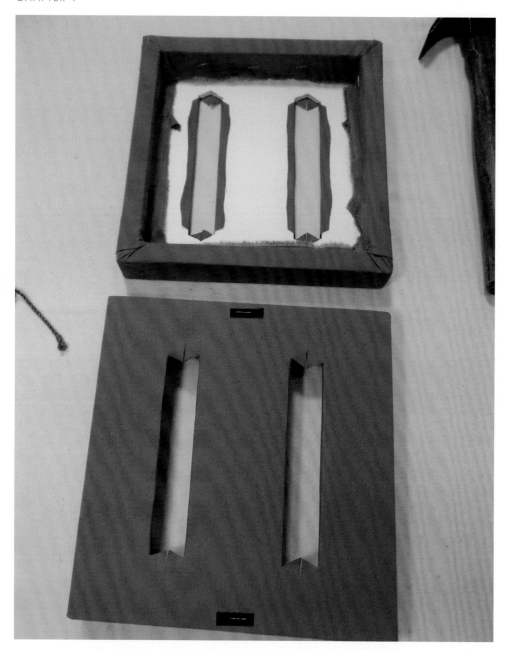

Front and back of frames with openings

Remember that you should always try to protect your tapestry. If you are mounting it over a simple frame, you should stretch at least one layer of sturdy fabric over the wood. This will protect your tapestry from the acids in the wood, and it will provide additional support for the work. If it is a large work, you might consider a layer of acid-free foam core board or thin plywood over the frame and under the fabric.

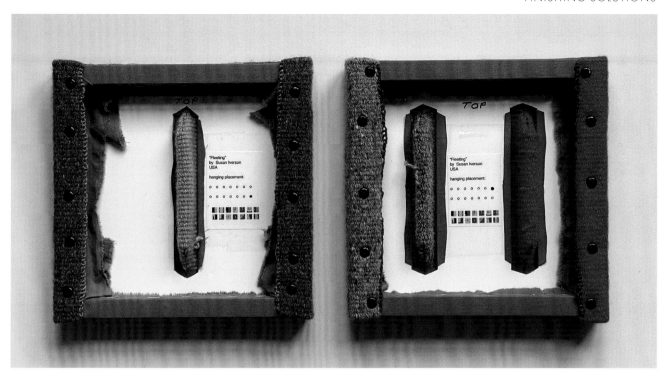

Backs of frames showing the inverted ridge coming through the opening. Note that information for installation has been attached to the back.

Front view of two of the fourteen panels

Penland Dawn, 2018. Tapestry, silk on cotton warp: approx. 2.5" × 4".

Back view of *Before the Stars*. Note that the two extra supports in the frame are placed so as not to interfere with the inverted ridges and to allow for a hanging wire.

Frames

In general, I don't like viewing my work with a visible frame. However, frames do have their uses. The primary functions of a frame are to protect the work and give it an environment that is complementary to the color, texture, shape, and size of the work, to make it look as good as possible. I frequently frame small tapestries to give them a quiet background and enlarge their presence on the wall. I stitch the tapestry to a heavy piece of printmaking paper and then put that in a deep frame. I prefer not to include glass unless it is really needed. The tapestry is protected but perfectly visible. If using glass, there are several types from inexpensive window glass to museum quality. Each type will reflect light differently. I would recommend that you get the best glass you can afford. You want to protect your work from UV light and other environmental conditions. For example, if you are selling work to a restaurant, glass will protect the piece from airborne grease and dust.

A Final Word on Finishing

All in all, finishing is simply solving the problems particular to each tapestry. You want your work to look as good as possible and to be presented in a professional manner.

I've shown you some of the solutions that work well for me, but they are certainly not the only possible solutions. Along with finishing your work appropriately for display, you should provide detailed installation information, with images if needed, when you send your work to an exhibition or to a new owner. What might seem obvious to you may be a mystery to someone who is handling your work for the first time.

DECIDING WHEN TO USE PULLED WARP (AN ARTIST'S JOURNEY)

Technique is just a tool. We all own a tool or two that works really well for what it is designed to do, but it is seldom pulled from the toolbox. Pulled warp is a tool like that. Learn it and explore its potential, and then put it in your technique toolbox until you really need it. It can partner with the idea behind your work to alter the form of your tapestry.

I was so fascinated by the idea of pulled warp in the 1970s that I assumed it would immediately influence my work and I would endlessly utilize its possibilities. That did not happen.

Fortunately for me, my ideas were stronger than my love of a specific technique. I let my sketchbook lead me. Whenever there was a sketch or idea that called for pulled warp, I would pursue it with more drawings and maybe a maquette. Some ideas made the cut and were woven; some did not. I learned to accept this.

I taught the technique, with great enthusiasm, to many students, and I continued to think about new ways to use it. It was exciting to see students experiment and then use the technique in ways I did not. I have used pulled warp in a fairly structural manner, while some of my students pushed it in a more organic direction. For the most part my ideas stayed at the "What if?" stage. As I was writing this book, I took the time to look back at some of my older sketchbooks. I was a little surprised to see how often I had included a pulled warp variation within the development of an idea. These variations ranged from reasonable to ridiculous. During this process I was following my own advice to investigate an idea thoroughly before moving on.

Aesthetic decisions are not always easy or even possible to fully explain. To help you in your own process, I will attempt to share with you some of the reasons why I used pulled warp for certain ideas and not for others. I

realize that these decisions have a lot to do with my love of the object quality of tapestries and my urge to increase that. Some ideas, generally the more narrative ones, demand to be flat on the wall, while others want to push into space and enhance their physical presence. I will talk with you about my tapestries in a roughly chronological way, but, for the sake of comparison, there will be some jumping around.

Early Work

Much of my work in the mid-1970s was built with multiple tapestry strips. These strips interwove with each other or were sewn onto a canvas backing (or both). They were soft yet structural. The strips cast shadows and pushed against each other, and I was satisfied with this level of physical dimension. I was investigating color and emotional states and trying, as a young artist, to figure out what my work was really about.

The yarn characteristics and color played a big part at this point in my development. Dyeing my own yarns was and continues to be an important aspect of my studio practice. I frequently needed multiple values of the same color, and that was impossible to find commercially. I was weaving with heavy yarns at a coarse sett and interested in the strong visuals of a composition built up on a grid system that remained obvious.

Calm Conversation, 1977. Tapestry, wool on linen warp: 5'5" × 5'5" × 1". *Private collection*

A Point in Time - Grey, 1976. Tapestry, wool and horsehair on linen warp: 5' × 5'.

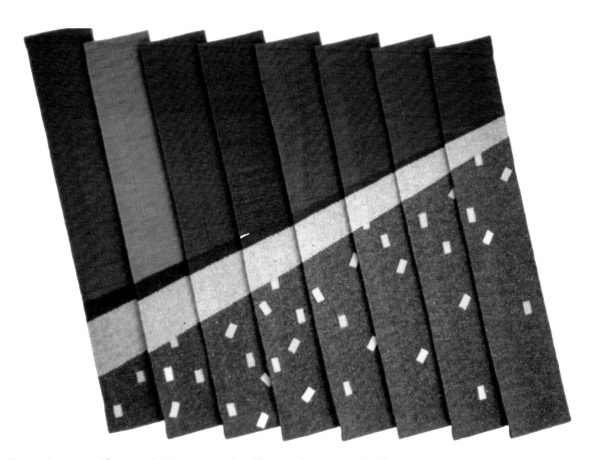

View - Momentary Glance, 1978. Tapestry, wool and linen on linen warp: 4' × 6'.

Notes Series

Language and marks that reference language make regular appearances in my work. *Notes*, one of my early series, specifically used the V and X shapes as compositional planes on which additional information appeared. I was more interested in the idea of communication, rather than the specific message. I was truly excited when I realized that the V-shaped tapestries could be woven using the pulled warp technique. As I mentioned in the preface, I had some technical difficulties in moving my ideas from small samples to large work, but after I got that worked out, I found the technique to be a good partner in this process. It allowed the V shapes to be as clean and sharp looking as the X shapes. Only a weaver, looking carefully at the Vs, would realize that something technically unusual was going on. I did find it wonderfully gratifying to finally use the pulled warp technique in a meaningful manner that I felt was true to the idea.

Notes - V-1, 1979. Tapestry, wool on linen warp: 6'6" × 6'3".

Notes - V-1 (detail), 1979. Tapestry, wool on linen warp: 6'6" × 6'3". The first of my V-shaped pulled warp tapestries.

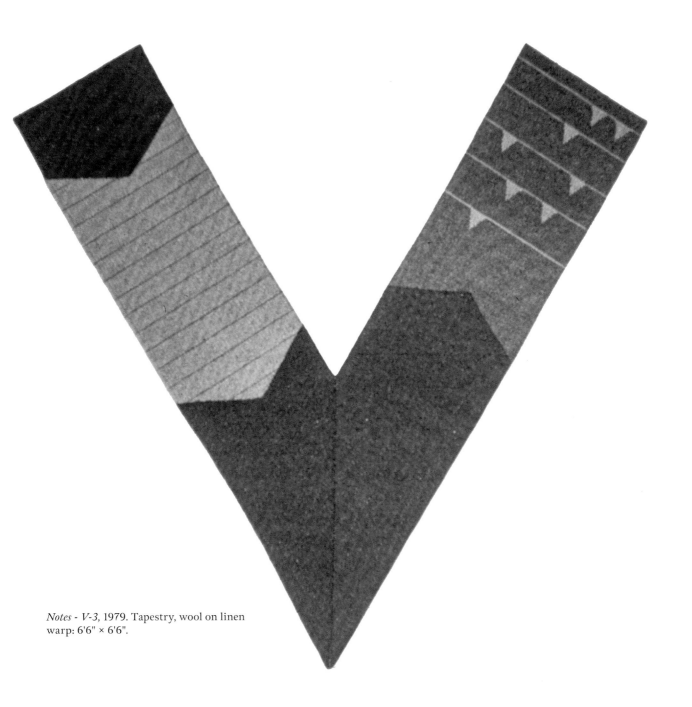

Notes - V-3, 1979. Tapestry, wool on linen warp: 6'6" × 6'6".

Notes - V-4, 1980. Tapestry, wool and silk on linen warp: 6'3" × 6'7".

Notes - X-1, 1980. Tapestry, wool and horsehair on linen warp: 8'2" × 6'.

Notes - X-4, 1980. Tapestry, wool on linen warp: 7'1" × 6'1".

Installation shot of *Susan Iverson / John Hawthorne,* an exhibition at the ICA Gallery of the Virginia Museum of Fine Arts, Richmond, Virginia, 1981

Notes - X-4 (detail)

View Series

In the 1980s I wove several series that had to do with ideas about moving through multiple environments, and the relationship between architecture and nature in the urban landscape. Doorways and passages were frequently featured in the compositions. I finally felt that I understood some of the ideas behind my work and the images that inspired them. I knew that composition and content were, for me, vital partners. None of these tapestries used pulled warp. They were composed of multiple, overlapping strips. Some tapestries were installed on the wall with horizontal and vertical strips, mimicking post-and-lintel construction.

Gates of Heaven - Portals of Pity, 1982. Tapestry, wool on linen warp: 6'9" × 3'6". *Private collection*

Passage - The Dead of Night, 1984. Tapestry, wool on linen warp: 6' × 7'. *Photo by Katherine Wetzel*

View Confinement, 1986. Tapestry, wool on linen warp: 5' × 7'. *Photo by Katherine Wetzel*

Peruvian-Influenced Series

At the end of the 1970s, I went on a life-changing trip to Peru. I left the US with a strong interest in Peruvian textiles but returned completely enthralled with the ancient textiles, architecture, and amazing landscape of Peru. The visual information I took from Peru was powerful and compelling, but I could not seem to get it down on paper in a way that did it justice. I felt inspired, but it took several years before my ideas for specific tapestries were fully realized.

Finally, in the mid-1980s my thoughts gained clarity, my sketches solidified, and I embarked on a large series. Along with the images of Peru, I was strongly influenced by the idea that the ancient textiles I was looking at had been made, sometimes used, buried with the dead, and then dug up by archeologists and grave robbers hundreds of years later. The level of abstraction in the imagery of some of these textiles was incredible and made me think more deeply about the evolution of contemporary abstraction.

Like much of my work since 1982, many tapestries in this series were composed of several strips that hung horizontally on the wall and overlapped each other by a couple of inches. While primarily flat, the overlapping panels cast shadows, and I felt that this gave them the required physicality I was seeking. I had been interested in the relationship between the human body and my work for years. This idea was most apparent when the tapestries were large enough to give the viewer the sense that they could step into the image. For that reason I requested that those specific tapestries should be hung only 1' or less off the floor.

Like many artists, I believe that my work already exists somewhere, in the ether, invisible, but waiting to be found. My role as an artist is to capture this work, this intangible idea, and give it a tangible life. I draw it, working on sketches until I discover the complete image.

Passage - Paracas to Ica, 1984. Tapestry, wool on linen warp: 6' × 7'. *Photo by Katherine Wetzel*

View - The Room of Flames, 1987. Tapestry, wool on linen warp: 3' × 8'. *Private collection; photo by Katherine Wetzel*

Ancient Burial V - Flutter of Wings, 1990. Tapestry, wool on linen warp: 6' × 7'6". *Courtesy of VCU Health; photo by Katherine Wetzel*

Ancient Burial VI - Night Secrets, 1990. Tapestry, wool on linen warp: 6' × 7'6". *Photo by Katherine Wetzel*

Night View Series

This series investigated the forms and colors that we see, or think we see, in low-light situations. The tapestries are about experiencing landscape and architecture at dawn, dusk, and night, when our sensory perception relies less on vision and more on hearing. Sounds and forms are altered as our imagination is allowed to react, and can easily override what we know to be real. Shapes that reference language and communication occur in most of these works. While the tapestries in this series have many similarities in materials, format, and size with the previous series, the palette is distinctly different. While dyeing all these yarns, I developed a strong love of chromatic grays.

It had now been over ten years since I had used pulled warp in my large tapestries. As in much of my earlier work, this series relied on overlapping panels or visual overlapping of shapes to enhance the physicality of the tapestry.

Night View - Ancient Message, 1992. Tapestry, wool on linen warp: 6' × 8'. *Photo by Katherine Wetzel*

Night View - Sounds of Night, 1993. Tapestry, wool on linen warp: 4' × 8'. While this is a single-panel tapestry, the image of three horizontal bands in the background is a reference to the overlapping tapestry panels in the other work. *Photo by Katherine Wetzel*

Night View - Secrets, 1993. Tapestry, wool on linen warp: 6' × 8'. *Photo by Katherine Wetzel*

Horizon Series

This series initially developed from a large number of small sketches done while I was still working on the *Night View* series. They included undulating surfaces that referenced draped or folded fabric. I knew right away that pulled warp could be a good match for the forms I was interested in creating. I made the conscious decision to alter some basic aspects of my work. I wanted to include yarns that were more reflective, as I thought that they could more accurately reference both water and the sky. I also wanted to work on a smaller scale. Many of my earlier tapestries had been in the 5' × 7' to 6' × 8' range, with some larger commissions. As my sketches progressed to cartoons and maquettes, I realized that many of these tapestries would work best if they had a rigid support behind the tapestry. I hadn't done that with previous work. Change is good, sometimes difficult, and sometimes almost effortless. I found this series to be very energizing, and as it grew, the ideas solidified. All the tapestries in this series investigate different horizon lines, and all but two use pulled warp in some way.

Horizon - Atlantic reveals my love of the ocean, daydreaming, and fabric. At its heart, it is about the feeling you get when you quietly observe the horizon line as the waves roll in. You relax, your mind might wander, and you are transported to another time or place. It is a creative moment. In the tapestry, you don't know if the "curtain" is going up or down or holding steady. What you do know is that you are getting a glimpse of something beautiful. In the past, the tapestries that were built with multiple, overlapping strips were still quite flat. The physicality of this tapestry was pushed to a different level by allowing the top layer to become dimensional through pulled warp.

This series includes tapestries with vertical ridges, vertical flaps, and ripples. The primary materials are linen and silk. Almost all the yarns were hand-dyed or the natural color of the fiber. I developed a new love of hand-painting dye onto silk and developing soft variegations of color on the skeins.

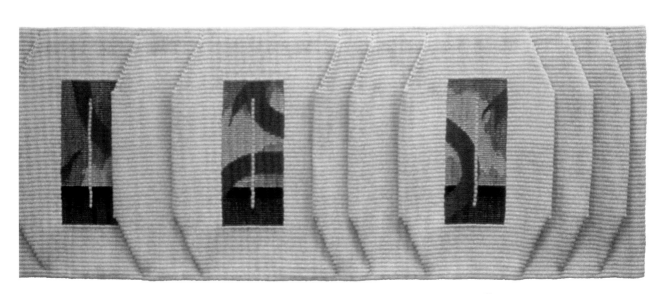

Horizon - The Road, 1997. Tapestry, linen and silk on linen warp: 23.5" × 61" × 5". *Private collection; photo by Katherine Wetzel*

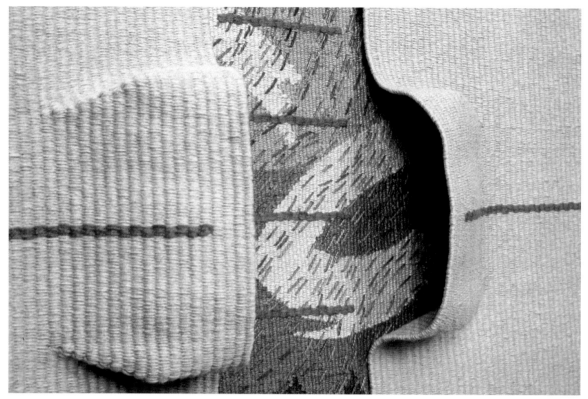

Horizon - Red Line (detail)

Horizon - Red Line, 1997. Tapestry, linen and silk on linen warp: 18" × 66" × 6". *Photo by Katherine Wetzel*

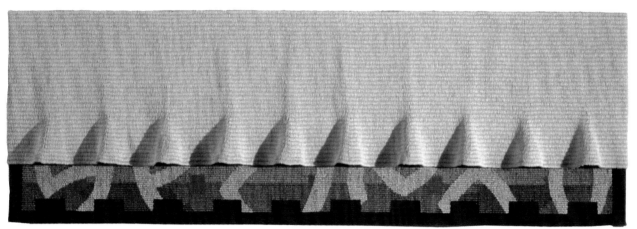

Horizon - Atlantic, 1997. Tapestry, linen and silk on linen warp: 20.5" × 62" × 5". *Courtesy of the Avenir Museum of Design and Merchandising, Colorado State University; photo by Katherine Wetzel*

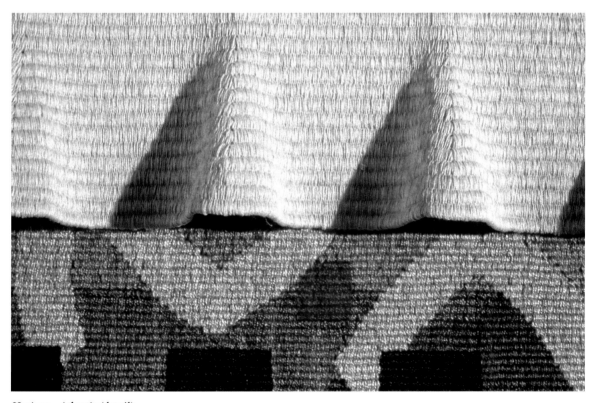

Horizon - Atlantic (detail)

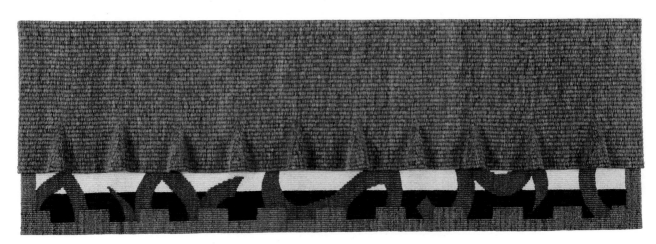

Horizon - Dawn, 1997. Tapestry, linen and silk on linen warp: 20.5" × 62.5" × 5". *Photo by Taylor Dabney*

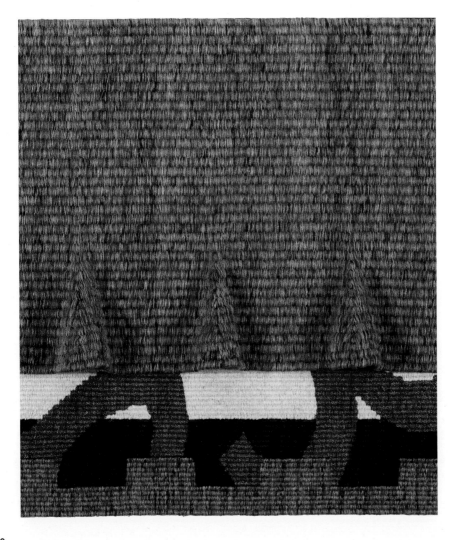

Horizon - Dawn (detail)

Horizon - Dusk, 1997. Tapestry, linen and silk on linen warp: 34" × 36" × 6".
Photo by Katherine Wetzel

Horizon - Dawn's Dance, 1998. Tapestry, linen and silk on linen warp: 25" × 63.5" × 3". *Private collection; photo by Katherine Wetzel*

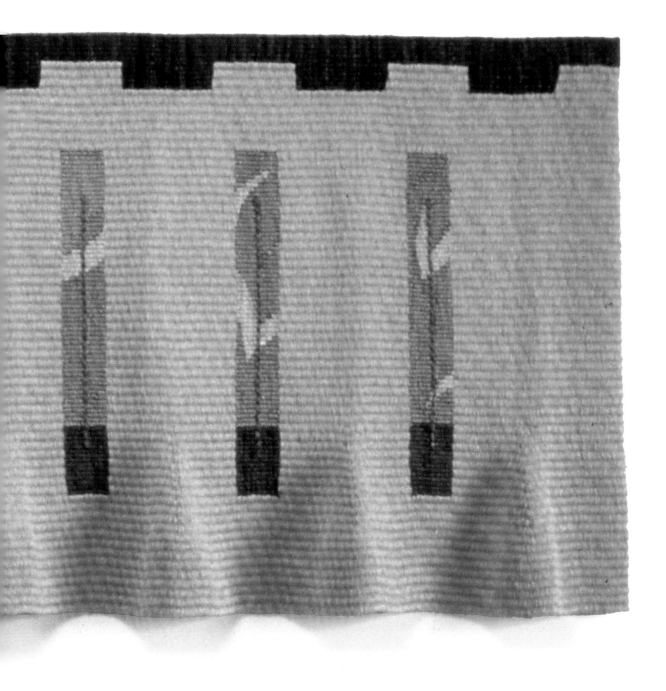

Horizon - Night, 1998. Tapestry, linen and silk on linen warp: 25" × 57.5" × 4". *Photo by Katherine Wetzel*

Horizon - Night (detail)

Giving free rein to intuition and my subconscious when thinking and drawing has allowed new ideas to take form. I trust this process. But it is not an "on demand" process; it requires time. It also requires editing. I freely move forward and backward in my sketchbook, drawing new ideas and revisiting and revising older ideas. This helps me see which directions have more lasting interest.

If you are having difficulty developing ideas, my main advice is to sketch. First, set yourself up for success by creating an environment that is conducive to creative work. Everyone is different, so you will need to figure out what works best for you. Sketch as often as you can, drawing small thumbnail sketches that relate to each other, but also vary. Try different formats. An image in a vertical format may just sit there, but the same image in a horizontal or square format might come alive. There are so many solutions to each visual question, and these sketches will help you hone in on an answer. An idea, floating around in your head, may seem brilliant, but get it down on paper (or screen) before you decide. For 40 years I told my students that if you can't draw it, you can't weave it. Of course, there are always exceptions, but I stand by my advice for most artists.

Great technique is wonderful, but ideas, concepts, or inspirations are what give heart to your work.

Horizon - Red Sky at Morning, 1999. Tapestry with linen, silk, and alpaca on linen warp: 25" × 65.5" × 3".
Photo by Katherine Wetzel

Horizon - Red Sky at Morning (detail). Pulled warp was also used to bend some of the arms of the small X-shaped tapestries that are appliquéd onto the surface. *Photo by Katherine Wetzel*

Horizon - Birth and Death, 2000. Tapestry, linen and silk on linen warp: 23.5" × 35.5" × 4". *Private collection; photo by Katherine Wetzel*

Horizon - Birth and Death (detail)

Horizon - Heaven and Hell, 2000. Tapestry, linen and silk on linen warp: 23.5" × 35.5" × 4". *Private collection; photo by Katherine Wetzel*

Right: Horizon - Desert Fire, 2000. Tapestry with wool, linen, and silk on linen warp: 30" × 36" × 4". *Photo by Taylor Dabney*

Dreams and Twins

As the *Horizon* series was ending, I realized that a simple silhouette of the head and shoulders of a person was appearing in my sketches on a regular basis. My work had been mostly nonfigurative up to this point, but I decided to push this idea and see what would happen. I wove two small tapestries with the figure included, and saw the potential. This opened the door to a flood of ideas that would eventually lead naturally into my *Twins* and *Dreams* series. At the very end of the *Horizon* series,

I wove several tapestries that I consider to be bridge tapestries, those that have one foot in the previous series and one foot in the next. Eventually I returned to the use of flat tapestry as my primary technique. I had become enamored with the rich colors and the soft luster of silk, and I continued using it as a primary yarn in the *Twins* tapestries. In the *Dream* tapestries, silk was frequently used to depict the dream imagery, while soft, gray wool became the night surrounding the figures.

Horizon - Dreaming the River God, 2001. Tapestry, linen and silk on linen warp: 24" × 63" × 3". This tapestry bridges the *Horizon* series and the *Dream* series. *Photo by Taylor Dabney*

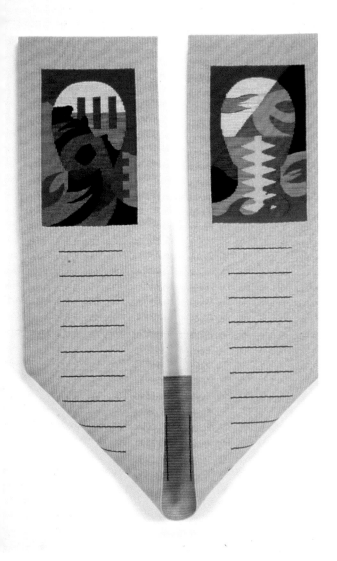

Horizon - Good & Evil, 2002. Tapestry, linen and silk on linen warp: 59" × 39.5" × 2". *Photo by Taylor Dabney*

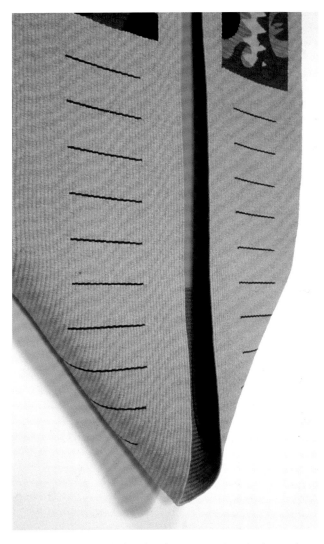

Horizon - Good & Evil (detail). This tapestry is a single panel that is simply folded. *Photo by Taylor Dabney*

The River Twins, 2003. Tapestry with wool, silk, and linen on linen warp: 36" × 55.5". The first of the *Twins* series. *Photo by Taylor Dabney*

"The nature of dreams and the process of dreaming intrigue me to the point of obsession. The separation between the real world and our dream world is sometimes thin. I am interested by both the similarities and the differences in these two worlds and vainly try to make sense of them."

(from artist's statement)

Useless Dreams I - VI, 2003–2004. Tapestry with wool, silk, and linen on linen warp: 36" × 29" × 2". *Photo by Taylor Dabney*

My sketchbook from this time period includes a number of drawings that investigate dimensional ideas, including pulled warp. The tapestries in both these series were more narrative in nature, and the images were generally best read in a flat format. Many of these ideas were simply made more confusing by adding pulled warp. There are always exceptions, and a few of these dimensional ideas were eventually woven. *Useless Dreams,* a series of six tapestries that are best hung together, used pulled warp in what I consider to be a psychologically disturbing manner.

Useless Dreams (side view). *Photo by Taylor Dabney*

141

Dream Sequence, 2007. Tapestry with wool, silk, and
linen on linen warp: 32" × 6'7.5". *Photo by Taylor Dabney*

*"The image of twins, two people so similar yet so
individual, may also represent the varied aspects
of the same individual. The silhouettes of these
twins are surrounded by their dreams or by a
landscape that merges with them."*

(from artist's statement)

The Third Twin, 2004. Tapestry with wool, silk, and linen on linen warp: 36" × 55.5". *Private collection; photo by Taylor Dabney*

The Sleeping Twin, 2005. Tapestry with wool, silk, and linen on linen warp: 34" × 65.5". *Photo by Taylor Dabney*

Our brains are quite amazing, open to learning, full of interests, laden with fears, able to feel immense joy and deep despair, and prodding us with memories. The brain is our best friend on some days and our worst enemy on others. My work grows out of my obsessions. But why I become obsessed with certain topics eludes me. I have learned to accept this, not to rush the internal timetable of the obsession, but to accept the validity of the ideas formed in my subconscious. I embrace them. I have faith in my brain to create work that is honest to me. Sometimes I, and my conscious brain, just have to get out of the way.

All that said, I still have moments or days of aesthetic angst. I can feel abandoned. The inner voice is quiet, and I rave about never having another idea. This passes.

Observations

In 2007 we moved from a very comfortable and convenient life in a suburb of Richmond, Virginia, to 10 acres in the country near the small village of Montpelier. While it was only 30 miles from Richmond, each day when I got home from teaching at VCU, I felt like I was on a different planet.

My initial work in this new environment was a continuation of the *Dream* series, with a stronger emphasis on human/environmental issues. I loved being surrounded by nature, but the rhythm of my life had changed so dramatically that it took awhile to settle in and to truly sort out my thoughts.

Almost every day I would take at least a short walk along the pond and through our woods. These walks, meandering through the woods, looking up at the treetops and down at the forest floor, allowed me to settle into my surroundings. They also provoked a new kind of curiosity about my environment. It was the nature of these walks that inspired the *Observation* series. The first in the series was really a bridge tapestry linking the *Dream* series to what would come next. It was composed of three sections that combined several different ideas all held together by the idea of time. It also employed pulled warp and embroidery. This was my first tapestry that included a significant amount of embroidery.

"I have become an obsessive observer of this world. Life on a secluded, woodland pond provides countless opportunities to observe both major and minor events. The sense of place and my attachment to the environment are major aspects of this work. I am influenced by both the physical landscape around me and the remembered landscapes that haunt me."

(from artist's statement)

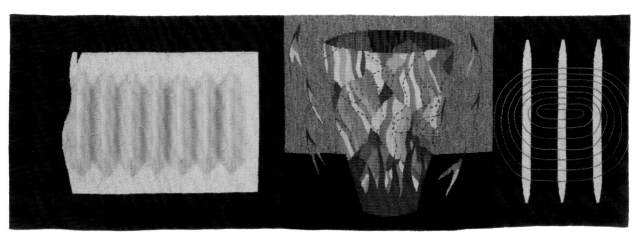

Seven Days at Millfield Pond, 2009. Tapestry with embroidery, wool, silk, and linen on linen warp: 23.5" × 71.5" × 2". *Photo by Taylor Dabney*

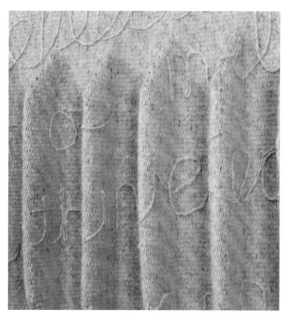

I was pleased that pulled warp was again an element in my work, and I used it in several additional tapestries. My work took on a clarity, but I was still slowly feeling my way forward.

Seven Days at Millfield Pond (detail), 2009. I was able to do some of the embroidery before the warp was pulled. The embroidery over the edges of the ridges had to be completed after the warp was pulled and the tapestry became dimensional. *Photo by Taylor Dabney*

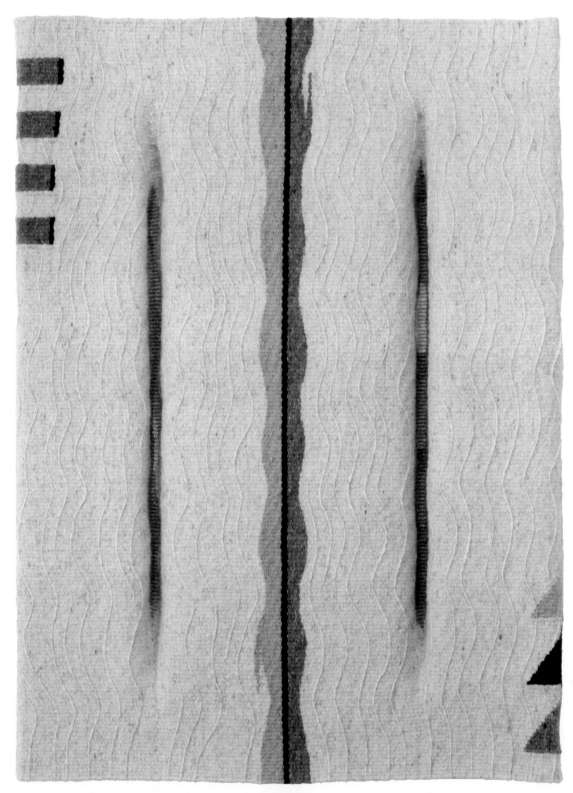

Beneath the Surface 2, 2010. Tapestry with embroidery, wool on linen warp: 33.5 × 24.5 × 2". *Photo by Taylor Dabney*

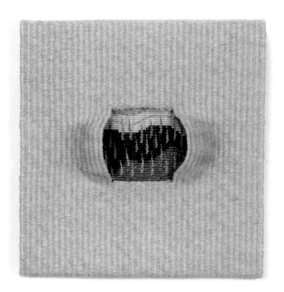

The Pond, 2009. Tapestry with embroidery, linen, and silk on linen warp: 4 panels 13.5" × 13.5" × 3.75" each. One panel is in a private collection. *Photo by Taylor Dabney*

Architecture is the first thing I remember looking at with a critical eye for the aesthetic and the practical. The daughter of an architect / structural engineer, I was taught the importance of structural integrity and structural beauty at a tender age. I have spent much of my adulthood slowly learning that the early lessons are the longest lasting. These lessons are so deeply ingrained that it has taken me a long time to separate them out into conscious thought. I was also taught that the landscape, humble or magnificent, was the ideal for beauty and surpasses anything humans can construct. These two things, architecture and landscape, which I avoided as individual areas of study in school, eventually became the primary sources for much of my work. I think of architecture as vertical and landscape as horizontal, much like weaving, two elements interlacing and building a whole out of the parts.

At this point in time I was sketching a lot, and much of it seemed chaotic. I was sorting out just how this new visual experience with the world would affect my ideas. While I had always hiked and spent a fair amount of time out of doors, I had lived in locations where there was a visual balance between architecture and nature. Architecture as a reference had always been a major factor in my work. In our new home, each window provided a view of only nature. We could see no other structures. This altered my work. I continued with ideas that had to do with walking through nature, but the format changed.

The new tapestries were both vertical and horizontal. They were composed of long, thin tapestry strips whose ends attached to the wall. This allowed the center of the strip to drape down, sometimes almost to the floor. Each work had multiple strips, and each strip could be considered a portion of a walk. These tapestries were dimensional and curved without the need for pulled warp. I loved the directness of this work, the simplicity of form, along with the complexity of the larger composition of multiple strips. The form also showed both the front and back of the tapestry strips, allowing the viewer to see the dimension of the fabric and to understand that the images on the front were also on the back.

Evening Rhythms (side detail), 2013. Tapestry with embroidery, wool and silk on linen warp: 30.5" × 62" × 8". *Private collection; photo by Taylor Dabney*

Winter Walk, 2010.
Tapestry, wool on linen
warp with frosted glass:
5'4" × 2'7" × 6". The glass
was commissioned.
Photo by Taylor Dabney

Verdant, 2010. Tapestry, wool on linen warp with glass: 4'3" × 7'4" × 6".
The glass was commissioned. *Photo by Taylor Dabney*

I felt that I could weave tapestries in this format forever. As in the past, when I became too comfortable with my work, I knew it was time for a change. True to form, the ideas in my sketchbook had already begun a transformation. Instead of looking down, I was looking up.

The Surface, 2010. Tapestry, wool on linen warp: 4'9" × 6' × 10".
Observing the ever-changing surface of the pond each day has
enriched my understanding of the visual connection between water
and the environment that it reflects. *Photo by Taylor Dabney*

Observations - Light

A big part of observing nature also involves looking at the sky. In the early to mid-1990s, I worked on *Night View*, a series that dealt with observing the world at twilight— dawn or dusk. Because of the darkness of these large wool tapestries, it was easy to portray the sky simply through softly muted colors. In 2014 I was again looking at the sky. Specifically, I was looking at sunrise and sunset, when the quality of the light shifted and the sky would frequently put on a fleeting show of vibrant color. I wanted to capture the sheer joy and awe provoked by these visual experiences.

In this body of work, color was primary and dimension was secondary. I did use pulled warp in many of these tapestries, but generally in a more subtle manner. Because the sky is endlessly deep, it made sense for me to invert ridges to create depressions where the color could seem to fold into the tapestry. With one large tapestry, *In the Ether*, I returned to the simple format of the original *Observation* series, but on a grander scale. It is specifically about the night sky and how we feel as we look up into it, remembering the magical moments of transition just before the deeper darkness descends. This tapestry also alludes to my belief that there are ideas floating in the ether, ideas that can connect or affect large groups of people during a specific time period.

Each of the tapestries in this series had specific needs related to scale and dimension. What holds them together as a series is the underlying concept. Visually the strongest connection is color, especially the bright pink.

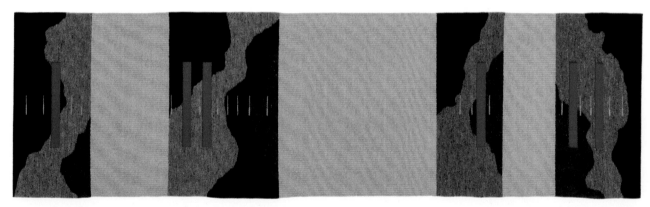

Transitory, 2015. Tapestry with wool, linen, and silk on linen warp: 30" × 8'9".
Photo by Taylor Dabney

Lingering, 2015. Tapestry with wool, linen, and silk on linen warp: 29" × 8'5.5".
Photo by Taylor Dabney

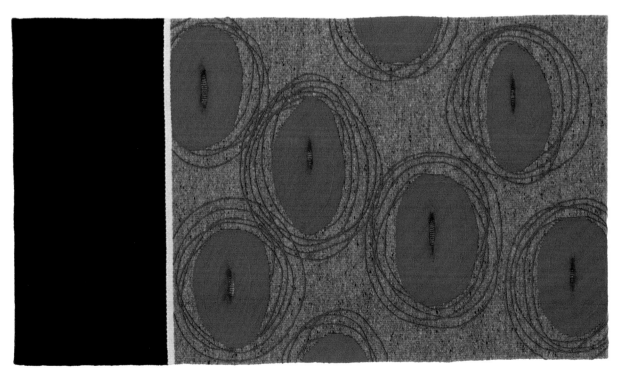

Before the Stars, 2018. Tapestry with embroidery, wool, silk, and synthetic
metallic floss: 25.75" × 45.5" × 2". *Photo by Taylor Dabney*

Fleeting (detail). *Photo by Taylor Dabney*

Fleeting, 2015. Tapestry with wool, silk, mohair, and linen on linen warp: installed, 24" × 7'10" × 2"; each panel 10" × 10" × 2". *Photo by Taylor Dabney*

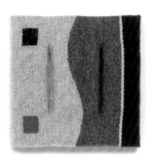

Pulse, 2019. Tapestry and embroidery with wool, silk, and synthetic metallic threads on linen warp: 23.5" × 31.5" × 2". *Photo by Taylor Dabney*

In the Ether, 2019. Tapestry, wool and silk on linen warp: 7'10" × 10' 3.5" × 8". *Photo by Taylor Dabney*

Right: *In the Ether* (side detail). *Photo by Taylor Dabney*

The Color of No, 2014–2019. Tapestry, wool and silk on linen warp. Installed at the Visual Arts Center, Richmond, Virginia. *Photo by David Hale*

While I was working on the *Observation - Light* tapestries, I also wove between 40 and 50 tapestries for *The Color of NO*. I considered these more of a single project rather than a series. These tapestries were always designed to be seen in a large group. Investigating the meaning of color and language, they are meant to provoke conversations about how we currently view the meaning of color in our society. I explored how and why color can affect a single word. I was interested in the experience we have as we engage with these simple ideas when an entire wall or an entire gallery is filled with these tapestries in different configurations. The tapestries are meant to be easily read, to converse with each other and with the viewer. For me, that meant that being flat was part of the concept.

All Things Equal

All Things Equal involves the use of the equal sign and other simple mathematical symbols that are used to ask questions about the visual information in each tapestry. *Building Night,* the first in the series, is another bridge tapestry. So far, all these tapestries lie flat against the wall. But who knows what will come next?

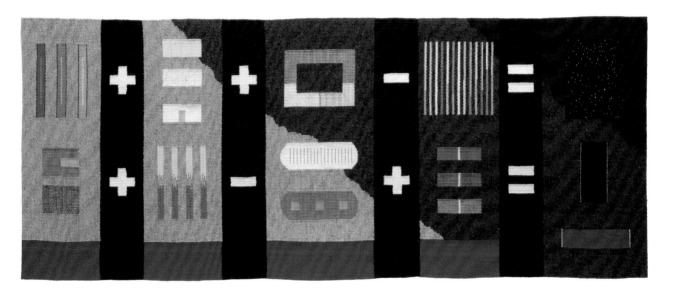

Building Night, 2019. Tapestry with wool, silk, and linen on linen warp: 28" × 5'10". *Photo by Taylor Dabney*

"These tapestries speak to the long history of humans and their relationship to each other and to the environment through thousands of years of development."

(from artist's statement)

Building a World (All Things Equal), 2020. Tapestry with wool, silk, and linen on linen warp: 28" × 52". *Photo by Taylor Dabney*

All Things Equal - The Beginning, 2020. Tapestry, wool and silk on linen warp: 32" × 55.5". *Photo by Taylor Dabney*

During the course of writing this book, along with weaving the samples, I decided to weave two small pulled warp tapestries. The first, *Magenta Morning*, was a prototype for a larger tapestry that I may or may not ever weave. The other, *Twilight's Passing*, was woven after I started wondering why I had never used loops in any of my work, even though I find myself drawn to the idea of them. Now that I have woven a tapestry with loops, I do want to weave more. The future is always a wonderful "What if?"

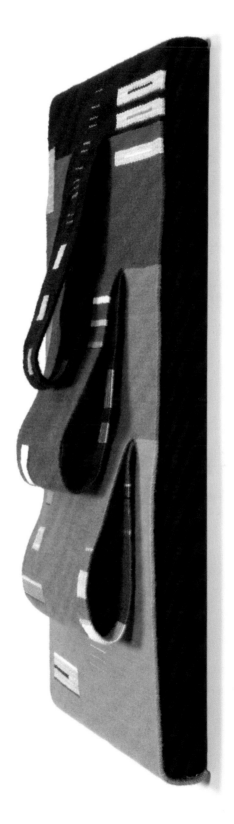

Twilight's Passing, 2022. Tapestry, wool and silk on linen warp: 30" × 18" × 5". *Photo by Taylor Dabney*

ACKNOWLEDGMENTS

There are so many people to thank for helping me in so many different ways during the course of my career that ultimately led to this book.

Particular thanks to:

Herman Scholton, whose beautiful and inventive tapestries started my curiosity in this technique that eventually led to the writing of this book.

My forever supportive brother, who bought me my first loom, a small Macomber, and then loaned me the money to buy my first Gilmore loom.

My amazing sister-in-law Francie, who is also a weaver and a dear friend, for her constant support and her hours of work reviewing this book.

My friend Ginger Thomas, who encouraged me before, during, and after the book-writing adventure. She was endlessly supportive and worked tirelessly reviewing this book.

Friends and colleagues Susan Brandeis, Tommye Scanlin, and Catharine Ellis, each of whom encouraged me to take on this project and who had the faith in me that I could get it done. Their advice and support have been priceless.

The many students who took a pulled warp workshop with me or who sat in on a presentation about the technique, showed their enthusiasm, and then requested a book. My special appreciation goes to the students in my 2018 class at Penland, who were bright, charming, funny, and, most of all, eager to learn. It was a privilege to work with each of them.

All the people at Schiffer who worked on this book, especially Sandra Korinchak, whose thoughtful and supportive editorial guidance has been invaluable. The design work of Ashley Millhouse brought the book to life.

The artists who kindly shared their work for this book: Adela Akers, Nicki Bair, Barbara Burns, Fiona Hutchison, Laura Meyers, Paola Moreno, and Sue Weil.

The many teachers and professors I interacted with who shared their passion and expertise on a daily basis. They taught me how to learn and how to teach and find joy in that process.

My students at Virginia Commonwealth University: the ones who followed all of my advice, the ones who followed almost none of my advice, the ones who asked so many good questions, the ones who struggled and struggled but prevailed in the end, the ones who found art making as easy as breathing, and the ones who were so good at making but have chosen a different path in life, I thank you all. A special thanks to my former graduate students, whose passion, energy, and talents have been a privilege to observe.

My parents, who were always there for me and gave me the gifts of a childhood laced with encouragement and a college education.

Friends who have graciously put up with my inattention during the writing process.

My husband, Ed Parsons, who for years and years has put up with my constant state of preoccupation, my hours in the studio, and my fits of "I'll never have another good idea." He was very helpful with the editing and photography for this book, and was always able to help me keep things in perspective. He delights in saying that it is his job to provide the "artistic angst" in my life.

ADDITIONAL ARTISTS TO LOOK AT

These are a few of the artists who have created work using the pulled warp technique, each using it in a unique way to bring dimension to their tapestries. I hope you will take the time to investigate their work further.

Adela Akers

You can learn more about Adela at
www.browngrotta.com

Adela Akers. *Summer & Winter,* 1977. Tapestry, linen warp and sisal weft: 84" × 72" × 10". The warps were pulled sequentially to form circles. Six panels hang vertically to form a cascade of folds. *Courtesy of the artist*

Barbara Burns. *Little Devil Corset*, 2018. Tapestry at 14 epi with pulled warp: 9.25" × 9.75" × 8". *Courtesy of Barbara Burns*

Barbara Burns

You can learn more about Barbara at

www.Burns-Studio.com

Instagram: burns.studio

Facebook: Burns Studio Tapestry

Fiona Hutchison

You can learn more about Fiona at
www.fionahutchison.co.uk
Instagram: fionahutchisontapestry

Fiona Hutchison. *Broken Tide,* 2020. Woven and manipulated tapestry, linen: 10" × 11" × 2". *Photo by Fiona Hutchison*

Laura Meyers. *Collapsed Geometries #1–5,* 2018. Pulled warp, silk and wool: 6' × 6' × 9'. *Courtesy of the artist*

Laura Meyers

You can learn more about Laura at

www.randommeanderings.art

Instagram: @less_random_meanderings

Paola Moreno. *Color Andino*, 2021. Tapestry with pulled warp, linen warp, and weft: 40" × 40" × 3". A series of 25 bowls inspired by the traditional textiles of the Andean region. *Courtesy of the artist*

Paola Moreno

You can learn more about Paola at
Instagram: spaolamorenom

Sue Weil. *By Land and By Sea*, 2020. Tapestry, cotton and wool on cotton warp: 20" × 30". *Courtesy of the artist; photo by Jay Daniel, Black Cat Studio*

Sue Weil

You can learn more about Sue at
www.sueweilart.com
Instagram: www.sueweilart.com

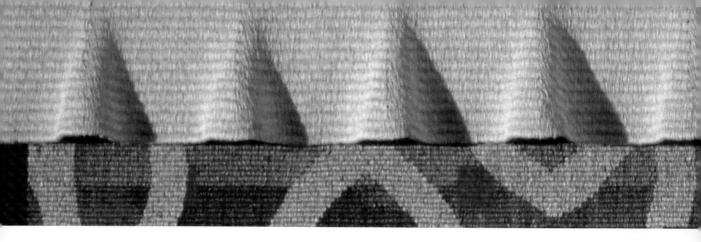

BIBLIOGRAPHY

Chandler, Deborah. *Learning to Weave*. Rev. ed. Loveland, CO: Interweave, 1995.

Collingwood, Peter. *The Techniques of Rug Weaving*. New York: Watson-Guptill, 1969.

Constantine, Mildred, and Jack Lenor Larsen. *Beyond Craft: The Art Fabric*. New York: Van Nostrand Reinhold, 1972.

Emory, Irene. *The Primary Structures of Fabrics: An Illustrated Classification*. New York: Spiral, 1966.

Larochette, Jean Pierre, and Yadin Larochette. *Anatomy of a Tapestry: Techniques, Materials, Care*. Atglen, PA: Schiffer, 2020.

Mezoff, Rebecca. *The Art of Tapestry Weaving: A Complete Guide to Mastering the Techniques for Making Images with Yarn*. North Adams, MA: Storey, 2020.

Scanlin, Tommye McClure. *Tapestry Design Basics and Beyond: Planning and Weaving with Confidence*. Atglen, PA: Schiffer, 2021.

Soroka, Joanne. *Tapestry Weaving: Design and Technique*. Wiltshire, UK: Crowood, 2011.

Todd-Hooker, Kathe. *Shaped Tapestry*. Albany, OR: Fine Fiber Press, 2004.

GLOSSARY

cartoon: The full-scale drawing for your tapestry

dart: A triangular or picket-shaped open warp area

header: The extra weft yarns at the beginning and end of a weaving that are used to space out the warp yarns and to hold the wefts in place during the pulling process. They are generally removed during the finishing processes.

maquette: A model of your pattern

pattern: The line drawing on paper that diagrams where you weave and where you will have open warp. This is usually placed behind the warp during the weaving process.

picket: A spacer that is shaped like a pointed fence picket

pulled warp: The technique where some areas of warp are left unwoven, and when the tapestry comes off the loom, this unwoven warp is pulled through the tapestry and out through the hem edge. (Historically this term was occasionally used to describe the look of wedge weave, but it did not describe the actual weaving technique.)

selvedge: The edges of the fabric that run parallel to the warp

spacer: Heavy paper that holds the unwoven spaces open

tapestry: A strict, technical definition is this: a weft-faced plain weave with discontinuous wefts.

thumbnail sketches: Small, quick sketches that help you get ideas down quickly. Mine are generally in the 1"–3" range.

warp: The vertical threads that are supported by the loom. In tapestry the warp is generally completely covered by the weft yarns.

weft: The horizontal threads that weave across the warp

Magenta Morning, 2022. Tapestry, wool and silk on linen warp: 10.5" × 10.5" × 3". *Photo by Taylor Dabney*

Images that have influenced me

ABOUT THE AUTHOR

Susan Iverson began weaving in college. She has an MFA from Tyler School of Art at Temple University and a BFA from Colorado State University. She was a professor at Virginia Commonwealth University in the Department of Craft/Material Studies for 40 years and has taught all levels of textile classes. She has held workshops on the pulled warp technique, including at Penland School of Craft, and has used it widely in her work as a studio artist. Her art has been exhibited widely throughout the United States and in Canada, Italy, Poland, Australia, and Uzbekistan. Her tapestries are in many collections, including the Art in Embassies Program, Capital One, the Avenir Museum (CO), and the Renwick Gallery at the Smithsonian American Art Museum in Washington, DC. Iverson lives and works in rural Virginia.

www.susaniversonart.com
Instagram: susaniversontapestry